"*A Citizen's Guide to U.S. Elections* fills an important gap in electoral studies. It manages to be part user's guide and part call to action, while at the same time maintaining objective and scholarly standards. Each chapter discusses perceived problems, evaluates existing evidence, and offers suggestions for concerned citizens. This book is perfect for the undergraduate classroom, community groups, or the general public. Bottom line: if you need a good grounding in the problems and potential of the U.S. electoral system, this is the book for you. I can't wait to use it in my classroom!"

Thomas M. Holbrook, *University of Wisconsin-Milwaukee*

"Jam-packed with crucial information about contemporary politics and elections, this terrific primer should be required reading for serious students and citizens who want to understand the electoral process and back up their opinions with facts."

Charlie Cook, *Cook Political Report* and *National Journal*

"This is not just a guide, but a perceptive, accessible synthesis of politics and political science. It explores the pressures, patterns and motivations that drive our electoral outcomes—and can change them. It's enlightening, a great read for political junkies, and a good one for any citizen who cares about democracy and each individual's capacity and responsibility to make a difference."

Robert M. Shrum, *University of Southern California; Senior Advisor, Gore 2000 and Kerry 2004*

"*A Citizen's Guide to U.S. Elections* offers a broad and engaging overview of elections in the U.S. The brief text provides students with a basic overview of electoral politics, situating the discussion in light of important scholarship by political scientists. It also challenges students to engage in a broader discussion about how citizens might engage to improve elections if they are dissatisfied with the current state of democracy in the U.S. A valuable contribution at a time of high levels of cynicism and negativity in politics!"

Jan Leighley, *American University*

A CITIZEN'S GUIDE TO
U.S. ELECTIONS

Political observers routinely lament that American democracy is broken, and many of them blame electoral malfunction. But is the system really broken? Panagopoulos and Weinschenk make the case that citizens are empowered to fix what's wrong with electoral politics and renew democracy in America, all within the institutional setup and framework of the existing system. Put simply, much of what is broken can be fixed if people stop throwing up their arms and start rolling up their sleeves to do the hard work of building our democracy. This book provides an overview of the basic features that characterize contemporary elections in the United States and includes discussions about voter participation and decision-making patterns, money in elections, and the role of parties and the media in presidential, congressional, and state and local races. It also outlines some of the most important trends and challenges in the current system. As a call to action, each chapter features potential solutions to the challenges that currently exist in U.S. elections.

Costas Panagopoulos is Professor of Political Science and Director of the Center for Electoral Politics and Democracy and the graduate program in Elections and Campaign Management at Fordham University.

Aaron C. Weinschenk is Assistant Professor of Political Science at the University of Wisconsin-Green Bay, where he teaches classes on American government and politics, Congress, public policy, urban politics, and statistics.

CITIZEN GUIDES TO POLITICS AND PUBLIC AFFAIRS

Morgan Marietta and Bert Rockman, Series Editors

Each book in this series is framed around a significant but not well-understood subject that is integral to citizens'—both students and the general public—full understanding of politics and participation in public affairs. In accessible language, these titles provide readers with the tools for understanding the root issues in political life. Individual volumes are brief and engaging, written in short, readable chapters without extensive citations or footnoting. Together they are part of an essential library to equip us all for fuller engagement with the issues of our times.

Titles in the series:

A CITIZEN'S GUIDE TO U.S. ELECTIONS

Empowering Democracy in America

*Costas Panagopoulos and
Aaron C. Weinschenk*

Routledge
Taylor & Francis Group

NEW YORK AND LONDON

First published 2016
by Routledge
711 Third Avenue, New York, NY 10017

and by Routledge
2 Park Square, Milton Park, Abingdon, Oxon, OX14 4RN

Routledge is an imprint of the Taylor & Francis Group, an informa business

Library of Congress Cataloging in Publication Data

Panagopoulos, Costas. & Weinschenk, Aaron C.
A citizen's guide to U.S. elections: empowering democracy in America / by
Costas Panagopoulos and Aaron C. Weinschenk.
    pages cm. (Citizen guides to politics and public affairs)
Includes index.
    1. Elections—United States. 2. Voting—United States.
    3. Democracy—United States. 4. Political campaigns—United States.
    5. United States—Politics and government.
JK1976.P32 2016
324.973—dc23   2015036584

ISBN: 978-1-138-85878-7 (hbk)
ISBN: 978-1-138-85879-4 (pbk)
ISBN: 978-1-315-71771-5 (ebk)

Typeset in Adobe Garamond Pro
by codeMantra

Printed and bound in the United States of America by Publishers Graphics,
LLC on sustainably sourced paper.

CONTENTS

FIGURES

FIGURES

TABLES

FOREWORD

Many of the common complaints about American elections have the same root: a deficit of citizen engagement in our democracy. This singular observation frames the lucid description and clear diagnosis of our electoral process offered in *A Citizen's Guide to U.S. Elections*. Is our electoral system broken beyond repair, or is the pessimism born of this argument one of the sources of the trouble? In addition to explaining the several facets of our complex system of elections—including the roles of money, interest groups, parties, and the media—the volume examines what has gone wrong and why. Perhaps as important as those observations is an assessment of how the problems can be addressed *within the existing system of institutions*. At the heart of the volume is this insight: the origins of our problems are in large part the low levels of participation undertaken by most citizens, whether voting, or campaigning, or protesting, or simply caring about and discussing politics. Armed with this insight, each chapter concludes with concrete proposals for meaningful participation within the current system. American democracy and elections surely aren't perfect, but the system provides the tools with which to strengthen these processes. The greatest needed reform may focus on the citizens rather than the system, encouraging greater engagement through the many opportunities our institutions provide. This volume offers Americans an understanding of elections and of their role in them; in this sense it is a true citizen's guide designed to empower democracy in America.

For a book of this nature we turned to two outstanding thinkers and teachers in American politics. Costas Panagopoulos—a graduate of Harvard and NYU, now the Director of the Graduate Program in Elections and Campaign Management at Fordham University—employs his personal experience as a campaigner, candidate, and commentator in addition to his impressive range of scholarship on U.S. elections (published in several academic journals, including the *American Journal of Political Science*, *Journal of Politics*, *Presidential Studies Quarterly*, *Electoral Studies*, *Public Opinion Quarterly*, *Political Psychology*, *Political Behavior*, *White House Studies*, and the *Journal of Political Marketing*). He is the author of previous books on campaign finance, online politics, interest groups, and the 2008 presidential election. In addition, he has served as the Editor-in-Chief of *Campaigns & Elections*, the preeminent journal for political consultants. His partner on this volume, Aaron Weinschenk, is a rising scholar of American elections, currently teaching at the University of Wisconsin, Green Bay. His research has been published extensively in scholarly journals such as *Electoral Studies*, *State & Local Government Review*, *Political Research Quarterly*, *Political Behavior*, *Presidential Studies Quarterly*, *American Politics Research*, and the *Journal of Elections, Public Opinion and Parties*.

Along with Panagopoulos and Weinschenk, we hope this volume encourages citizens to realize—as the authors so aptly phrase it—that it is time to stop throwing up our arms and start rolling up our sleeves.

Morgan Marietta & Bert Rockman
Series Editors

ACKNOWLEDGMENTS

Although there are just two names on the cover of this book, this project would not have been possible without the support of many more individuals.

Costas thanks his family, Mark and Benson, and his colleagues and collaborators, as well as the numerous teachers, mentors, and students who generously imparted their wisdom about campaigns and elections over the course of many years. Published nearly a quarter-century after his 1992 run for the Massachusetts state legislature, this volume also provides an opportunity to offer a special note of gratitude to Claudette Houle, his campaign manager, and to the many advocates and volunteers and, crucially, to the voters of the 17th Middlesex district in Massachusetts at the time who supported his campaign and who taught him more about the electoral process than any book or article.

Aaron would like to thank the Department of Political Science at the University of Wisconsin—Green Bay. His colleagues were incredibly supportive, and he couldn't ask for a better department. He also thanks his students, with whom he shared many of the ideas discussed in this book over the past several years. He appreciates his students for continually pushing him to explain things in a clear and accessible way. Aaron also thanks friends and colleagues, Tom Holbrook, Katia Levintova, Chris Terrien, Tim Lynch, Zach Wallander, and David Helpap, for their support over the years and as he worked on this project. Tim and Rhonda Weinschenk and Bob, Lori, and Kyle Gassenhuber also deserve special thanks. Finally, he thanks his wife Katie. She is, quite simply, the best. Without her love, support, and encouragement, this project would not have been the same and may not have been finished in as timely a manner as it was. He thanks her for always asking how the book was coming along. Happily, he can now report that it is done!

ACKNOWLEDGMENTS

The authors would be remiss if they did not thank Morgan Marietta and Bert Rockman, the editors of this series, and the team at Routledge. Their thoughtful comments were invaluable as this book developed, and it was an absolute pleasure to work with them.

NOTES ON THE AUTHORS

Costas Panagopoulos is a leading expert on campaigns and elections, voting behavior, media and public opinion, political psychology and campaign finance, Professor Panagopoulos has co-authored or edited several books, including *Politicking Online: The Transformation of Election Campaigns Communications* (Rutgers University Press) and *Public Financing in American Elections* (Temple University Press). He has published over 60 scholarly articles in outlets including the *American Journal of Political Science, Journal of Politics, Public Opinion Quarterly, Political Behavior, Political Psychology,* and *Political Analysis*. He is editor of *American Politics Research* and has also served as Editor-in-Chief of *Campaigns & Elections* magazine, as Senior Editor of the *Journal of Political Marketing,* and as part of the NBC News Decision Desk team since the 2006 election cycle. He has also been a Visiting Professor of Political Science and a Research Associate at the Center for the Study of American Politics and the Institution for Social and Policy Studies at Yale University and has taught at Columbia University and New York University. In 1992, while an undergraduate at Harvard University, Professor Panagopoulos was a candidate for the Massachusetts State Legislature.

Aaron C. Weinschenk is an expert on voting behavior, campaigns and elections, mayoral politics, public opinion, and political psychology and has published over a dozen journal articles in outlets such as *Political Research Quarterly, Political Behavior, American Politics Research, State and Local Government Review, Electoral Studies,* and the *Journal of Elections, Public Opinion, and Parties*.

1

INTRODUCTION

Politics is about power. In a democracy, elections are the mechanism by which power is retained by the people. In representative democracies, elections ensure that power is transferred into the hands of the people or parties that citizens believe will represent their interests in government. When elections malfunction, the very essence of democracy is threatened.

Many political observers routinely lament that American democracy is broken. It appears that most Americans agree: A CNN/Opinion Research Corporation poll conducted in 2010 asked a representative sample of citizens whether they thought "our system of government is broken," and a whopping 86% of respondents said that it was.[1] In a 2011 poll conducted by *The Washington Post,* 78% of people said that they were dissatisfied with "the way this country's political system is working."[2] Although these polls did not ask people why they felt this way, it seems quite reasonable to think that, for many people, a great part of the blame for the broken system falls on the way elections are conducted in the United States. Indeed, most Americans can probably rattle off a list of the things they don't like about elections with a great deal of ease—campaigns are too negative, candidates and parties are too polarized and combative, candidates seem disconnected from ordinary citizens, incumbents continually win reelection when fresh faces and new ideas are needed in government, wealthy campaign donors and special interest groups have an excessive amount of influence over candidates and elected officials, candidates waste too much money on campaigning, the two major political parties unnecessarily limit the choices people have during elections, it's hard to know where to get good political information, and the list goes on and on. It seems unlikely that these problems will go away after the elections end and politicians transition from campaigning to governing.

In light of these complaints, various institutional reforms have been proposed to "fix the broken system." In this book, we ask a simple question: *Is the system really broken?* Our answer to this question is one that is likely to evoke some controversy: *Not really.* Not really? But you just listed a host of problems with our current system! Our answer is based on this argument: *Although there may be many pressing issues and dissatisfaction with the electoral process, our system isn't really broken because it is currently within Americans' power to fix what's wrong with electoral politics (and politics in general) all within the institutional setup and framework of the existing system.* In other words, it may not be so much the system that's failing as it is a failure on the part of American citizens to take action to address the important concerns in our democracy—to consistently and meaningfully participate in the political process. We need to start taking full advantage of the *tools that our system of government offers* to produce the outcomes we desire. The beauty of a democracy is that citizens have the ability to govern themselves—to select and remove their representatives, to come together to solve collective problems, to voice their ideas and opinions—and yet, in the United States, citizens routinely bypass opportunities to participate in elections and politics. Many people complain about the political candidates who run in American elections or the lack of good ideas that politicians have, but how many people have worked for a candidate they supported or, better yet, run for elective office? Many people think that Congress is doing an abysmal job these days, but how many people have contacted their elected officials to voice their opinions? The answer to both of these questions, as you might suspect, is very few. Very few people take action on the problems or issues that they think are important. Although it's easy to blame the *system* for the problems mentioned above, we believe that *American citizens share in the responsibility.* Ordinary Americans don't participate much in elections and public affairs (levels of political engagement are especially low when elections are not occurring) nor do they invest in acquiring information about candidates, issues, and policies. When citizens aren't active players in the political process—when they aren't there to monitor what's going on, to hold elected officials accountable, and to express their preferences—it's not surprising that many of the problems we experience continue unabated or even worsen over time.

Although we agree that there are many important issues and concerns in the United States, we argue that most of what is "broken" can be fixed if people *stop throwing up their arms and start rolling up their sleeves* to start the hard work of renewing our democracy. Just to be clear, our argument is not that citizens are likely to rush to solve every

2

problem that they see or to address every complaint that they have. Our argument is that they *could* if they were willing to put in the effort. To be fair, we certainly acknowledge that citizens are not completely to blame for all of the problems that exist (there is rarely one single cause behind any given problem), but the lack of civic participation is part of the reason why politics has become so dysfunctional. It is interesting to note that in *The Washington Post* poll mentioned above, 77% of Americans agreed with the statement "Whatever its faults, the United States still has the best system of government in the world." And in the CNN poll mentioned above, 81% of Americans said that our system "can be fixed." The question is *How do ordinary citizens begin to address the challenges that exist, some of which seem insurmountable?* We certainly don't have all the answers, but we're convinced that Americans can be a big part of the solutions to many of the nation's political ills.

Before we describe how this book will unfold, we think it's important to take a moment to address some of the recent descriptions of American politics that have gained traction. Many political observers (and ordinary citizens) seem to believe that Americans are fairly powerless or helpless (or both) when it comes to politics. Indeed, many arguments have pointed out that politics and political issues are too complicated to understand or to participate in, that our government is so fragmented it's hard to know who's responsible for what, that congressional districts have been gerrymandered to increase polarization and reduce competition by ensuring that certain parties and candidates win, and that interest groups spend excessive amounts of money during elections and control political outcomes. These conditions mean that ordinary folks don't have much of a role to play in politics and that most things are beyond their control. We concur that many of these issues are distressing in the United States, but we disagree with the notion that citizens are powerless in our democracy. Quite the opposite, we believe that citizens can (and will have to) play a central role in resolving the things they think are so bad about American elections and politics. And, although citizens regularly complain about many of the features of our electoral system, we hope that in reading this book people will realize that *they actually already have the tools at their disposal to fix the things they dislike*. In short, citizens can operate successfully within the current system. A centerpiece of the existing political system is that it enables reform of institutions, processes, or behaviors—or all of the above if necessary. For example, if citizens are concerned about making sure that elected officials do a good job representing constituents, citizens can do more to increase monitoring (e.g., participate in elections, gather information about what elected officials are doing, contact elected officials, etc.). We do not necessarily need a new system; we can do plenty within our framework to improve the electoral process.

We want to make it clear that our argument does not imply that solving the problems we face will be easy. Many of the problems that Americans perceive regarding the practice of elections will take serious and sustained attention and action. Americans must recognize that democracy is not easy. If ordinary citizens are unhappy with what's going on and want something to change, they are obligated to take action. They carry much of the burden for creating political change. Think there's too much money in politics? Do something about it. Don't like the candidates who run for political office? Do something about it. Want elected officials to pursue a particular policy or address a particular issue? Do something about it. It's easy to complain about things, but complaints must be accompanied by action. Many people seem to have adopted the perspective that things are "too hard" or "impossible" to change. This perspective undercuts the essence of what it means to have a democracy. A democracy, unlike many other systems of government, enables ordinary people to govern and to make political changes. Although our political system may have features that make change difficult, it is certainly possible. One of the exceptional things about our political system is that the Founders were wise enough to know that while they didn't create a perfect system, it is a perfectible system. Constant vigilance, work, and reform are crucial to that enterprise. If citizens are unwilling to take action on issues they dislike, they may have to learn to live with the things about which they so often complain.

We believe that it is important to keep in mind that when public opinion is strong and clear, citizens have decisive influence, as political scientist Paul Burstein has noted.[3] In short, *intensity is the currency of American politics*. Although citizens can probably not have much influence on things like the fractured nature of American politics (e.g., the system of federalism that divides government into different layers), they can influence things like the degree of intensity and participation in politics. We think this is where election reform should focus. A number of questions follow from this idea. For example, how do we increase citizen interest and participation? How do we increase the proportion of issues on which citizens respond with intensity? Throughout this book, we offer some ideas to help address these questions.

This is a book about electoral politics in the United States. It is also a book about political representation. Many of the concerns people have about elections in the United States seem to revolve around whether they achieve representation in the way that was intended. We believe that elections are not only about political accountability—that is, holding elected officials responsible for what they achieve (or not) when in office—but they are also very much about political representation. Political scientist Robert Dahl[4] has noted that "a key characteristic of a democracy is the continued responsiveness of the government to the preferences of its citizens, considered as political equals." If elections are the means by which we select government leaders, then understanding elections is central to understanding responsiveness. Much of the discussion in this book focuses on the extent to which the conduct of elections in the United States and the behavior of citizens and elected officials thwart or enhance representation.

Indeed, many of the problems with U.S. elections that we have mentioned connect directly to the issue of political representation. If interest groups are playing too large a role in elections, does that mean that some people or groups are not being represented in government? If the parties from which we are electing candidate are too polarized, what does that mean for the policies we are getting out of government or for the ability of government to address policy problems that the general public believes need attention? If only certain groups of people participate in local elections, what does this imply about those whom elected officials will listen to once in office?

When thinking about representation, it is interesting to consider how much our political system was really intended to be representative. Interestingly, many of the features of our political and electoral system were actually intentionally built in by the Framers to *avoid* mass representation. It often shocks people to learn that up until the ratification of the Seventeenth Amendment in 1913, U.S. senators were actually elected by state legislatures and not by popular vote. The Electoral College, the institution that elects the president, was implemented because the Framers did not believe that ordinary citizens were educated enough to make such an important choice. Over time, the United States has evolved toward more and more representation, to the point that it is now most often assumed to be the clear goal. If we accept the idea that political representation is important—that elected officials should be responsive to the citizenry that elected them—then the fact that many people believe that U.S. elections are failing or are broken means that, to at least some extent, representation is being hindered (or that it is being subverted by money, special interest groups, etc.). In short, dissecting American elections can tell us a lot about the kind of representation we are getting (or are likely to get in the future). It may also be able to tell us about how we can do better.

This book departs from previous texts on elections in a number of important ways. First, this book is designed to provide a nontechnical introduction to some of the most important issues related to American elections. To that end, the chapters are written with a general audience in mind. We explain some of the basic features that characterize elections in the United States and outline some of the most important problems and challenges that exist within the current system. When appropriate, we clarify myths that people have about elections in the United States. Although many people have negative perceptions about the American electoral system, we adopt a more optimistic outlook in general. We cannot possibly cover every single aspect of U.S. elections, but we have tried to include major topics and issues.

Second, this book offers some ideas about potential solutions to the problems and challenges that are often associated with U.S. elections. Since our argument centers on the idea that Americans must play a role in fixing the things they do not like in our system (and that they can change things within the system we have), we believe that it is important to provide a set of ideas that may serve as a starting point for action. It's not possible to list every potential solution. That is not our goal. Instead, we hope that this book helps to start a dialogue about what can be done to improve American democracy and encourages people to reconsider their role in the political system.

This book features eight substantive chapters that cover what we see as some of the most important topics and questions when it comes to American elections. We begin in Chapter 2 with a discussion of voter turnout and political participation. Next we proceed to money, campaign finance, and the role of special interests in elections. The next three chapters present details about presidential, congressional, and state and local elections, respectively. Chapters 7 and 8 focus on two key institutional players in electoral politics (political parties and the media), and Chapter 9 focuses on vote choice. In the final chapter, we provide some parting thoughts on the future of American democracy. We begin with political participation because of the central role engagement plays in our electoral and political process. Let's get to it.

Notes

1. http://i2.cdn.turner.com/cnn/2010/images/02/19/rel4f.pdf.
2. http://www.washingtonpost.com/wp-srv/politics/polls/postpoll_080911.html.
3. Burstein, Paul. 2003. "The Impact of Public Opinion on Public Policy: A Review and an Agenda." *Political Research Quarterly* 56: 29–40.
4. Dahl, Robert A. 1971. *Polyarchy: Participation and Opposition*. New Haven, CT: Yale University Press.

2

POLITICAL PARTICIPATION

On November 12, 2013, voters in Crutcho, Oklahoma, went to the polls to vote on a school bond proposal. The election asked voters to cast a ballot either for or against a $980,000 bond to improve the local public schools. The proposition was approved by a margin of five votes. Amazingly, only five votes were cast in the election. Of the 927 registered voters in Crutcho, just five people showed up to vote! If you do the math, you find that voter turnout in this particular election was a meager 0.5%. That's an astonishingly small percentage of the pool of registered voters making a choice about a fairly large amount of public resources. As one journalist remarked after the election, "Depending on how you look at it, the bond proposal Crutcho voters considered Tuesday either sailed through or was approved by the narrowest of margins."[1]

Other stories related to low levels of citizen engagement in elections abound in the United States. During the June 2014 primary election held in California, for example, one polling place in Somona County, which theoretically serves thousands of registered voters who live in the precinct, literally did not have a single person show up to cast a ballot.[2] During the November 2013 mayoral election in New York City, the largest city in the United States, 24% of registered voters turned out—better than 0.5% turnout, but still not an overwhelming level of citizen engagement (and the lowest turnout rate in that city in the past 50 years).[3] Perhaps the most humorous example comes from a city council election in Missouri City, Missouri. In that election, one council candidate, who was running unopposed, "failed to win his reelection … Turns out, he didn't get any votes at all, not even one from himself. He later told reporters he had forgotten it was Election Day, as apparently did the other registered voters in his ward."[4]

We should point out that turnout rates in these examples are likely even lower than suggested. The statistics reported above use the number of registered voters as the denominator when calculating turnout rates. Using the number of registered voters actually inflates the turnout rate because it excludes the people who are theoretically eligible to vote but who are simply not registered. The number of *eligible voters* in a given place is almost certainly larger than the number of *registered voters*, so the real turnout rates (in places that calculate turnout as a percentage of registered voters) are often even lower than those reported. Although the levels of voter turnout mentioned above may seem abysmal, low levels of voter turnout in elections are actually the norm in the United States, as we will show in more detail as the chapter unfolds.

In this chapter, we provide an overview of trends in political engagement in the United States. We highlight patterns in voter turnout, the most basic act of political participation in a democracy, but also discuss trends in other political activities (donating, volunteering, displaying yard signs, attending meetings, etc.). We also provide an assessment of trends in online political participation. Americans have a wealth of opportunities at their disposal to choose elected officials, articulate their preferences and beliefs, and press for political representation and accountability. We highlight the fact that, although citizen engagement in politics and public affairs is extremely important to a healthy democracy, citizens regularly bypass chances to provide input into the political system. The problem is not that opportunities are lacking for citizens to partake in the electoral process; they abound in the United States. The problem is that many citizens choose not to participate. And low levels of political engagement are partly the cause of some of the problems we currently experience. Although citizens regularly complain about politics and elected officials, most citizens are not heavily involved in the electoral arena or in politics in general. Fortunately, low levels of citizen engagement in U.S. elections and politics can be remedied. At the end of this chapter, we provide a number of ideas about how to improve civic engagement.

The importance of enhanced engagement is a central theme in this book. All things considered, we believe greater public input in the electoral and political processes is a good thing, even if citizens do not always embody the ideal voter. But we acknowledge that not everyone agrees (and, as we discuss above, maybe not even the Founding Fathers!). Some are not troubled by limited engagement and participation in the political process. In fact, elitist approaches express skepticism about greater participation, often pointing to evidence that the public is typically too poorly informed on matters of public policy (more on this in subsequent chapters) and possibly too susceptible to manipulation by enterprising politicians. Supporters of a more elitist approach argue that these uninformed voters would only muck up the process. Overall, these concerns are legitimate, and they resonate in both academic audiences and the public at large. Clearly, the quality of democracy is strengthened when interested and informed citizens participate, while it can be degraded when too many participants are misinformed or manipulated. But we also believe there are consequences to anemic electoral participation— when too many citizens opt out of the process—effectively relegating electoral decision making to those most engaged (who are often those with the most wealth, power, and stake in the system). The preferences, and potentially even the wisdom, of these privileged few may not necessarily be superior to the broader citizenry. Moreover, it is hard to imagine that even those who subscribe to elitist viewpoints could justify low and ever-shrinking participation rates. What if only 5% or 10% participate in the process? As we describe above, such scenarios do occur, perhaps with greater frequency than we might imagine. Is this still a defensible level of participation? Would leaders truly have a mandate to govern? Where do we draw the line? Is there a point at which low participation becomes too low? And perhaps more importantly, who would draw the line? We adopt a more inclusive view of democracy, even if the end result is messier and flawed. To a great extent, we focus on describing the contours of the current electoral process in America with the hope of identifying opportunities for, and dismantling structural barriers to, a more informed *and* a more involved electorate. As we explain here, our view is that the current political and technological environments create unprecedented opportunities to achieve both.

Voter Turnout Rates

In the United States, citizens are generally fond of the idea of holding elections to make political choices. For many Americans, elections represent a fair and equal way of making collective decisions. Indeed, the principle of "one person, one vote," which suggests that each eligible voter must have his or her vote counted (regardless of who he or she is or what attributes he or she has), is one of the most important ideas in American politics. Elections also allow people to resolve their "biggest (and smallest) questions with ballots, not bullets."[5] They allow people to engage with their government. They provide a way for people to make their opinions heard. For many people, elections (and the expression

9

of opinions that they allow) are the essence of what it means to have a democracy. Indeed, the word "democracy" literally means "rule by the people," and free, fair, and frequent elections are an important component of democratic governance.[6]

The sheer number of elected positions signals the importance of elections to Americans. According to Table 2.1, the United States has 513,200 elected officials in total. Although elections for federal offices—the president of the United States and Congress—often attract the most media attention, the majority of the elected offices in the United States (99%) are actually at the state and local government levels—in states, counties, municipalities, townships, school districts, special districts, and state legislative districts across the country. Through participation in federal, state, and local elections, U.S. citizens have ample opportunities to express their preferences at the ballot box. One observer noted that "the average American is likely to be called to the polls more than twice a year, every year."[7]

Table 2.1 Number of Elected Officials in the United States

Level of Government	Number of Elected Officials
Federal Government	542
State Governments	18,828
Local Governments	493,830
Total Number of Elected Officials	513,200

Note: Data from U.S. Census of Governments, https://www.census.gov/prod/2/gov/gc/gc92_1_2.pdf.

Despite the importance placed on elections in the United States, it often surprises people to find out that Americans typically participate at relatively low rates. For those who are politically active (you know, the people who make it a point to vote in every election—whether it's for the president of the United States, the local dogcatcher, or the uncontested city council seat—come hell or high water), it is sometimes hard to imagine why others would not participate in the political process. Interestingly, even in the most salient elections—U.S. presidential elections—a large slice of eligible voters will fail to vote. Figure 2.1 provides a graph showing the turnout rates in presidential general elections over the period 1948 to 2012. Although the level of voter turnout has moved up and down over time (the average is 58.2%), at no point over the period we examine has presidential turnout exceeded 64%. Even when the turnout rate reaches its highest level, more than one-third of the electorate

10

is not registering its preferences on Election Day. To give you a sense of how many people do not participate in presidential elections, in the 2012 presidential election, there were 221,925,820 eligible voters in the United States and the overall turnout rate was 58.2%.[8] This means that 92,854,914 potential voters (41.8% of the eligible voting population) provided no input into the selection of the president of the United States. In some years, that figure is even higher.

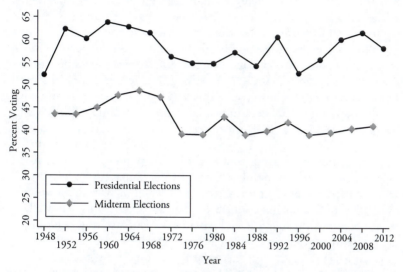

Figure 2.1 Voter Turnout in U.S. Presidential and Midterm Elections, 1948–2012. Data from United States Elections Project (http://www.electproject.org).

When it comes to midterm elections—elections held two years after the quadrennial elections for president—the turnout rate is typically much lower than it is during presidential election years. As Figure 2.1 illustrates, turnout in midterm elections has ranged from 39% to 49% over this period, with the average being 42%, or about 30% lower than in presidential years. Once again, we see that even in high-turnout years like 1966 when turnout was 49%, a majority of the electorate (51%) stays home on Election Day.

Given the trends shown in Figure 2.1, it is interesting to consider why, despite the increasing levels of education in the U.S. population over time, expansion of voting rights, and elimination of structural barriers like poll taxes and literacy tests in recent decades, turnout hasn't steadily increased. Political scientists Rosenstone and Hansen (1993) have pointed out that a decline in voter mobilization efforts (especially by parties and groups like unions) was one of the main reasons behind the decline in turnout in the United States between the 1960s and the 1990s. They note that if parties, unions, and other groups had put as much effort into voter mobilization in the 1980s as they had in the 1960s, voter turnout would have fallen by less than 3% rather than by the 11% that it did.

In Figure 2.2, we provide a look at the percentage of people who said that they had been contacted by either of the major political parties. It is interesting to note that although the percentage of people being contacted by the parties has never exceeded 43%, the number of people reporting contact from at least one of the parties increased beginning in 2000. In general, voter mobilization efforts tend to increase political engagement, and some evidence suggests the effects of grassroots mobilization efforts are actually getting stronger in recent cycles.[9] Political scientists Kenneth Goldstein and Travis Ridout point out, "If propensities to vote are not only determined by immutable demographic factors but by environmental and strategic factors as well, then reducing the structural barriers to voting and strengthening the amount or quality of mobilization may bring more people to the polls. In short, if the volume and quality of mobilization and voter contacts are a big part of the problem, perhaps improving the quality and increasing the volume of mobilization and voter contacts can be part of the solution as well."[10] A number of studies conducted by political scientists using randomized field experiments have put a wide range of grassroots mobilization strategies and tactics to the test in recent years and have identified several effective approaches.[11] Some of the most promising techniques tap into psychological mechanisms to stimulate participation and can be as simple as thanking voters for previous participation or for their political involvement.[12]

Clearly, as Figure 2.1 illustrates, there is considerable room for improvement in voter participation in national elections. Zooming in on the turnout rates in the most recent presidential elections (since 2000), however, provides some encouraging evidence and hints at the tantalizing possibility that an era of renewed engagement may be on the horizon. Voter participation in these cycles, and especially in 2004 and 2008, was comparable to turnout rates witnessed in the United States during the 1960s. While it is still too early to know if this pattern will be sustained (the dip in turnout in 2012 is a cautionary note), the data suggest, optimistically, that voter apathy is not on an irreversible, downward spiral; apparently, voters (still) have the capacity to be galvanized into action and successfully mobilized. Figuring out how to systematically induce greater participation is not easy, however. As we note above, political engagement has not always been as responsive as we might expect to institutional changes designed to stimulate participation. Nevertheless, here (and throughout) we offer some ideas about reforms that could potentially enhance citizen engagement in politics.

Figure 2.2 Percent of People Contacted by the Major Political Parties, 1956–2008. Data from American National Election Studies (http://www.electionstudies.org).

In state and local elections, turnout rates are often even lower than in midterm election cycles. This often comes as a surprise, especially when people find out that of the three levels of government in the United States (federal, state, and local), citizens generally express the highest levels of trust and confidence in local government. Indeed, a 2012 Gallup poll found that 74% of people expressed a great deal or fair amount of trust in local government. This level of trust in local government has been quite stable over the past several decades in the United States. Since Gallup has been asking survey respondents about trust in local government, trust has ranged from a low of 63% (in 1972) to a high of 77% (in 1998).[13] Presumably, these high levels of trust stem from the feeling that local governments are closer to home than the other levels of government and are therefore more likely to be responsive to citizens. Given that Americans tend to have favorable views of local governments, it seems natural to think that they would participate in local politics with high levels of enthusiasm. In reality, the opposite is true. Local-level races typically attract very little attention from voters. They are often low-salience events that attract little to no media attention and entail very little campaigning or political competition. While few cities have voter turnout levels as low as the 0.5% level in Crutcho, Oklahoma, studies have shown that turnout generally averages around 25% in mayoral and city council elections in the United States—with turnout rates in some cities sinking below 1%.[14] When it comes to other local elections, such as those for city clerk, treasurer, or school board, voter turnout often drops lower than 25%.

Primary elections, the elections held to select the candidates from each party who will move on to general elections, are one final set of elections worth considering. Primary elections tend to be low-salience events, especially when they are held for offices at the state or local level. Even at the federal level, though, turnout tends to be quite low. One report on the 2012 primaries noted that in the presidential and U.S. Senate primaries turnout was "the lowest on record, at 15.9 percent of eligible citizens."[15] Since 1998, average turnout in federal-level primary elections has not exceeded 20%.[16] Primary elections at the state and local levels typically attract very low levels of voter engagement. Many states have seen remarkably low turnout rates in recent state-level elections, with some states even hitting record lows.[17] Voters commonly express the view that it is not important to participate in primary elections, since the general election is what really determines the winner. This idea, however, fails to recognize that the candidates who participate in general elections are derived from primary elections. In short, primaries are remarkably important: Outcomes determine the candidates who will compete in the general elections that follow. Groups and individuals who do participate in primaries will have much greater influence in the selection of political candidates than those who do not participate. It makes sense that candidates are likely to pay more attention and be more responsive to those who participate in their selection and provide resources to their campaign.

While this book focuses on U.S. elections, we think it's important to provide a bit of comparative information on electoral participation. Although the evidence indicates that turnout rates for American elections tend to be low, it is possible to get a sense of how these turnout rates compare to turnout rates in other countries. One study on turnout in national legislative elections placed the United States 120th in its ranking of turnout rates across 169 countries.[18] It is important to note that some of the differences across countries stem from differences in institutional features. For example, some countries have mandatory voting and weekend voting rather than weekday voting. Countries that have mandatory voting consistently see higher rates of turnout, especially when the enforcement of compulsory voting is strict and penalties are high.[19]

Civic Participation Beyond Voting

The voter turnout patterns highlighted above are at odds with the ideas that many Americans seem to hold about the importance of using elections to select representatives and make other political choices. Many Americans would probably agree with the statement that ordinary citizens should be able to hold elected officials accountable by "throwing the rascals out" if they are not doing what the people want. Many Americans like the notion of contending ideas or candidates facing off against each other in an election. Many Americans believe that elections are an important way for people to express their preferences. Given these widespread beliefs about the importance and value of elections, why don't people vote in them at high rates? Perhaps Americans do not find voting to be the most appealing political act and turn to other kinds of political engagement to express their opinions, exert influence, and press for political accountability and political representation.

While voting is arguably the most basic political act in a democracy, it is certainly not the only way for citizens to participate in the political process. There are literally dozens of ways for citizens to get involved across the three levels of government in the United States. In Table 2.2, we provide information from a recent survey on the extent to which Americans participate in 15 different political acts beyond voting. Our data are from a nationally representative survey fielded in 2012, but data from surveys in other years show very similar tends.[20] The political acts considered in Table 2.2 range from things that can be done during an election season (e.g., attending a campaign rally) to things that can be done at any time on the political calendar (e.g., attending a city government meeting). When we investigated voter turnout rates in the United States, we found that participation in elections was not incredibly high. When it comes to other political activities, it turns out that Americans don't participate at very high rates either. Out of the political acts listed in Table 2.2, which is certainly not an exhaustive list, the act with the highest percentage of participation is talking to people about voting for or against a candidate or party. While 40% of people said that they participated in this activity, the majority at 60% reported not participating. The other political acts show even lower levels of participation. Virtually no one volunteers to work for parties or candidates, attends political meetings, rallies, speeches, or dinners, writes letters to newspapers or magazines about political issues, or gives money to political parties. Participation in all of the acts (besides talking to people about voting for or against a candidate or party) falls below 25%.

Table 2.2 Political Engagement Beyond Voting

Political Act	Did Participate	Did Not Participate
During the campaign, did you talk to any people and try to show them why they should vote for or against one of the parties or candidates?	40%	60%
… go to any political meetings, rallies, speeches, dinners, or things like that in support of a particular candidate?	6%	94%
… wear a campaign button, put a campaign sticker on your car, or place a sign in your window or in front of your house?	15%	85%
… do any (other) work for one of the parties or candidates?	3%	97%
… give money to an individual candidate running for public office?	11%	89%
… give money to a political party during this election year?	8%	92%
During the past four years, did you join in a protest march, rally, or demonstration?	6%	94%
… attend a meeting of a town or city government or school board?	18%	82%
… sign a petition on the Internet about a political or social issue?	24%	76%
… sign a petition on paper about a political or social issue?	23%	77%
… give money to any other organization (not counting a religious organization) concerned with a political or social issue?	24%	76%
… call a radio or TV show about a political issue?	3%	97%
… send a message on Facebook or Twitter about a political issue?	21%	79%
… write a letter to a newspaper or magazine about a political issue?	4%	96%
… contact or try to contact a member of the U.S. Senate or U.S. House of Representatives?	19%	81%

Note: Data from the 2012 American National Election Study.

It is interesting to note that political acts that rely on technologies like the Internet and social media also do not have high levels of citizen participation. About 24% of people have signed an online petition and about 21% have used Facebook or Twitter to send political messages.

Table 2.3 provides a more detailed assessment of the extent to which people use social media to engage in politics. Although the advent of new technologies has been heralded as something that might promote more civic engagement, the statistics shown in Table 2.3 do not signal that large numbers of people are using social media to participate in politics. Although there are certainly some people who engage in this way, the people who participate online tend to be the same people who are politically active offline.[21]

Table 2.3 Political Engagement via Social Media

Political Act	Percent of All Citizens Who Have Done This
"Like" or promote material related to political/social issues that others have posted	23%
Encourage other people to vote	21%
Post your own thoughts/comments on political/social issues	20%
Repost content related to political/social issues	19%
Encourage others to take action on political/social issues that are important to you	19%
Post links to political stories or articles for others to read	17%
Belong to a group that is involved in political/social issues, or working to advance a cause	12%
Follow elected officials, candidates for office, or other public figures	12%

Note: Data from Pew Research Center's Internet and American Life Project, July 16–August 7, 2012 Tracking Survey, N=2,253 adults ages 18 and older.

Figure 2.3 makes the point about low engagement even clearer. In this graph, we tallied up the number of political acts (out of the 15 possible in Table 2.2) that each person in the survey reported participating in and plotted the percentage of people who engaged in each number of political acts. It is clear from the graph that few people in the United States are very active in political and civic life. The percentage of people who engaged in more than five political acts is just 13%. The majority of Americans (63%) who participated in three or fewer political acts on average. In short, despite the wide range of political activities available in the United States, few citizens take advantage of the opportunities at their disposal to engage with politicians, candidates, and government.

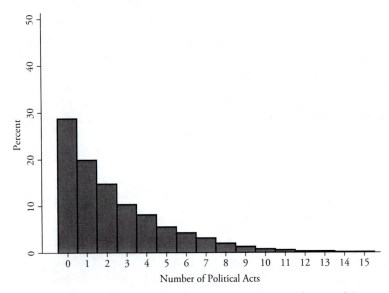

Figure 2.3 The Lopsided Distribution of Political Engagement in the United States. Data from the 2012 American National Election Study.

Who Votes?

In addition to examining the distribution of political engagement, it is important to consider the gaps in political engagement that exist in the United States. In Table 2.4, we provide a look at voter turnout by different demographic groups in the electorate in the 2008 general election. Consistent with numerous previous studies, we observe a number of disparities in turnout rates among different groups. Those who are 18 to 24 years old, for instance, voted at a much lower rate than those in all of the other age categories. In addition, less educated and less affluent Americans voted at much lower rates than those with greater educational attainment or income, respectively. Similar patterns have been routinely observed in previous cycles. Political scientists have long known that there are inequities when it comes to political engagement, and many have expressed concern about the extent to which inequities translate into unequal representation in government. A number of studies have shown that members of Congress are more responsive to the preferences of those with high incomes and education levels than those with low incomes and education levels.[22] To the extent that inequities in political engagement translate into inequities in political representation and public policies, there may be good reason to care about the participatory habits of different groups in society.

Table 2.4 Voter Turnout Rates by Group (2008 Presidential Election)

Group	Percent Voting
Men	62%
Women	66%
White alone, non-Hispanic	66%
Black	65%
Asian	48%
Hispanic (any race)	50%
18–24 years old	49%
25–34 years old	57%
35–44 years old	63%
45–54 years old	67%
55–64 years old	72%
65–74 years old	72%
75 and older	68%
Less than high school graduate	39%
High school graduate or GED	55%
Some college or associate's degree	68%
Bachelor's degree	77%
Advanced degree	83%
Less than $20,000 annual family income	52%
$20,000–29,999 annual family income	56%
$30,000–39,999 annual family income	62%
$40,000–49,999 annual family income	65%
$50,000–74,9999 annual family income	71%
$75,000–99,999 annual family income	76%
$100,000 and over annual family income	80%

Note: Data from U.S. Census Bureau, http://www.census.gov/prod/2010pubs/p20-562.pdf.

The Effects of Low Levels of Political Participation

There are a number of interpretations that could be made about the trends sketched out above. One interpretation is that there is no real problem. If voting is optional, then the turnout patterns we get are the turnout patterns we get, and we should not worry much about it. In other words, if only 0.5% of people want to vote in a school bond election, then let those people vote and let the other 99.5% of people stay home. If 75% of voters want to stay home when a city council election is happening, then let them stay home. Everyone has the chance to vote and if some people don't want to then why should we care? Maybe people don't vote because they're generally pleased with the political system (except that they routinely say they're not so pleased). These arguments seem intuitive for a lot of people. Although we see the reasoning behind these notions, we disagree with the idea that we should not care about the rates of participation in American elections (or other political processes). We also disagree with the idea that there is nothing that can be done to increase activism. The other interpretation that could be made about the above trends is that if elections (and other acts of civic participation) are one of the cornerstones of a democracy, then we should be quite worried that many citizens are not participating.

One of the things that the first interpretation misses is that low levels of political engagement are actually behind some of the problems that exist in our democracy. Here's a perfect example. One of the perennial concerns for ordinary Americans is the influence of special interest groups and lobbyists in our system. Indeed, a survey conducted in 2011 asked a representative sample of U.S. adults whether they thought lobbyists had too much power, about the right amount of power, or not enough power, and 71% of respondents said that lobbyists have too much power.[23] Citizens tend to dislike the idea that special interest groups are biasing the political system—pulling for outcomes that are out of sync with what ordinary citizens want, giving large sums of money to elected officials or helping their preferred candidates win elections, and, once elected, make policy. Although there is widespread agreement among citizens that special interest groups and the people who work for them are "bad," few people stop to think about the implications of low voter turnout for the influence of interest groups in American politics. One political science study recently showed that in low-turnout environments (like local-level elections), the largest and best-organized interest groups have increased influence and that the public policy that emerges afterwards tends to be more favorable to those groups. The logic behind this finding is quite simple. One of the strategies that interest groups use during elections is to mobilize, inform, and persuade voters. Those efforts are much more likely to have an impact on the election outcome when the baseline level of voter turnout is low.[24] Think about it: If turnout is really low, then the integration of even just a small number of voters (perhaps those who are mobilized by an interest group) to the election can have a supersized impact. In the context of the school bond election in Crutcho, Oklahoma, mentioned above, an interest group would literally need to mobilize just a few voters in order to skew the vote. In that election, five people turned out to vote, all of whom voted to approve spending nearly a million dollars. Had just six more people turned out to vote and all voted "no" on the proposal, the end result would have been much different. In line with this idea, another political science study pointed out that "there may be a limit to the number of constituents any elected official can reach and be responsive to, and these well-attended constituents could make up a larger share of the electorate where turnout is low" and found that cities that see low levels of voter engagement "have spending patterns that benefit particular subgroups in the population who have good reason to overcome high participation costs."[25]

Yet another example of how low turnout can create biases in our system comes from a political science study on political representation. The authors noted that "if almost everybody turns out, there can be very little skew. If, however, only a small fraction of the population turns out, skew can be severe" and found that "lower turnout leads to substantial reductions in the representation of Latinos and Asian Americans on city councils and in the mayor's office."[26]

Here's another example of how low turnout can have important effects on other aspects of our political system. We noted that primary elections often suffer from remarkably low voter turnout rates. One of the consequences of low voter engagement in primary elections is that these elections have become more driven by activists (people who participate with a lot of intensity). Activists tend to be more ideologically extreme than most citizens. The participation of activists in primaries (and the lack of participation by people who aren't activists) can reduce the influence of political moderates. It can also open up opportunities for moneyed interests to exert greater influence. One news article recently pointed out that "the influence of a few—liberal or conservative—would not be nearly so easy to achieve if more people voted in these races that often get little attention." Political scientist Michael McDonald went on to remark that, "Because people aren't tuned in, they don't see the importance of this until it bites them."[27]

As a final example of how low turnout can be problematic, it's interesting to think about the consequences of low turnout for incumbent reelection rates. In American elections (at all levels of government), incumbent candidates (those who already hold the elected position) are reelected at very high rates (typically 80–95% of incumbents are reelected). This is called the "incumbency advantage." It's interesting to note that low turnout can actually enhance the incumbency advantage. Indeed, one study found evidence in the context of city council elections that when voter turnout is high the electorate contains a larger number of unpredictable voters, who are less likely to have a connection to the incumbent. Thus, when turnout is high, it lowers the likelihood that incumbents can win reelection. Put another way, when voter turnout is low (and the electorate is made up of more reliable voters, who are more likely to have a connection to incumbents), incumbent candidates stand a better chance of getting reelected. The implication of turnout being related to incumbency in this way is that reelection may sometimes be achieved "regardless of their performance as representatives." This seems problematic from the standpoint of political accountability and political representation.

The above examples all make a similar point: When voter turnout is low, many of the problems that ordinary people often complain about (interest group influence, skewed public policies, inadequate political representation, polarized parties and candidates, incumbents continually winning) are actually worse than when voter turnout is high. Thus, although it is convenient to suggest that we should be unconcerned with rates of political engagement, it's critically important to recognize that low levels of political engagement are actually behind some of the problems that people are quite concerned about. In short, we ignore low levels of citizen engagement at our own peril.

Why Do People Participate (or Not) in Politics?

Given the importance of political participation in a democracy, it probably won't come as a surprise to learn that political scientists have devoted a great deal of attention to figuring out why some people participate while others do not. There are a number of prominent ideas about political participation that deserve attention. One of the most well-known theories about participation comes from Anthony Downs, who argued that when choosing whether to vote, potential voters calculate the expected utility (what they gain by the action) and vote if the benefits exceed the costs. The basic intuition here comes from economics and is rooted in rational choice theory, which proposes that people make decisions about consumer purchases by weighing the benefits against the costs. Political scientists have applied this reasoning to voting and many other forms of political behavior.

It is worth pointing out that for many people it may not take much for the costs of voting to exceed the benefits. Downs suggested that this problem can be represented by this equation: $R = (P*B) - C$. Here, R represents the net benefit (or, more technically, the expected utility) of voting, B represents the utility gain if their preferred candidate wins, P represents the probability that the individual's vote will yield the preferred outcome (the likelihood that the individual is pivotal), and C represents the costs of voting.

By this logic, potential voters participate if $R > 0$. Generally speaking, the probability of being the pivotal voter in an election is infinitesimally small in most elections. (In order for a single vote to change the out-come, the vote total would have to be tied or within one vote to begin with, which is extremely unlikely; otherwise one vote in practical terms would change nothing.) So even if the benefits of an election victory are meaningful, the value for $P*B$ in the above equation is likely to be zero or close to zero. Any real cost, then, overrides this gain and makes voting unbeneficial. It is important to think about what the costs of voting might entail. There are a number of factors that could make voting "costly": not just things that cost money (e.g., buying a newspaper to learn about political candidates) but also things that cost time. One of the costs is the investment that a voter makes before an election in acquiring information about the candidates, registering to vote, and so on. Another cost is the time invested to actually cast a ballot (e.g., traveling to the designated polling place, waiting in line to vote, and forgoing the other things that could be accomplished if an indi-vidual was not spending time voting). If citizens approach the decision to vote from this rational perspective, in which the costs of voting often exceed the benefits, this is a clear explanation of low voter turnout.

Although this theory is quite simple, it has been modified to account for an additional factor that might influence participation decisions. Political scientists Riker and Ordeshook (1968)[28] introduced a new item to the equation, so that it reads $R = (P*B) - C + D$, where D rep-resents the benefits that one gets from expressing oneself or performing one's civic duty. According to this idea, D might be shaped by perceptions of appropriate behavior (e.g., social norms and conformity to the expecta-tions of others), personal psychological factors (e.g., sense of civic duty), or solidarity or purposive benefits (the satisfaction derived from work-ing with like-minded people or toward a policy goal, respectively, even if the goal is not achieved). Importantly, in the new voting equation, the benefits that are associated with the D term grow even if an individual's vote is not pivotal. Thus, the D term, unlike the effect of the B term, does not decline due to the fact that the value of the P term is typically quite small. If the second equation—representing a more psychological or soci-ological approach to voting—is more accurate than the purely rational approach of the first equation, then this opens up new ways of thinking about what would influence citizens to increase their participation. In a section below, we will illuminate how this theory of voting can help us think about some possible solutions to low voter turnout.

Another prominent idea about why people participate (or not) focuses on the role of resources. According to Brady, Verba, and Schlozman (1995)[29], decisions to get involved in or stay away from politics revolve

23

around three sets of resources—time (to participate), money (to donate to political candidates, parties, and causes), and civic skills. Civic skills refer to communication and organizational abilities (e.g., the ability to speak in public, to write well, to lead groups, etc.) that are helpful for people to have when they are engaging in political acts. Brady et al. demonstrate that these resources play an important role in shaping the intensity people bring to politics and the kinds of participation they choose. Importantly, Brady et al. demonstrate that some people—those who are socioeconomically advantaged—are more likely to have the time, money, and civic skills that can lead to biases in rates of political participation. Once again, this idea about why some people participate and some people do not can help us think about some possible solutions to low citizen engagement in politics.

Following recent elections, the U.S. Census Bureau has queried Americans about their voting practices and probed respondents who indicated they failed to vote about their reasons for doing so. Table 2.5 presents the results from the Census Bureau's Current Population Survey conducted after the presidential election in November 2012. The reasons Americans themselves provide for not voting in the election reflect many of the considerations discussed above. Most Americans (19%) who failed to vote in the election did so because they were too busy or had conflicting schedules. About 16% said they did not vote because they were not interested, and 14% claimed illness or disability. Nearly 13% confessed they simply didn't like the candidates or the campaign issues. Other reasons included being out of town (9%), experiencing registration (6%) or transportation (3%) problems, or even bad weather conditions (1%); 3% of respondents indicated they abstained because the polling place was inconvenient to get to. Astonishingly, nearly 4% of respondents confessed they simply forgot to vote!

Clearly, there are some things (the weather, illness, disability, or forgetfulness) that will be difficult to address in order to boost participation, but we could adopt reforms to mitigate the effects of other impediments. We discuss some of these ideas here, adding that we could improve access to voter registration, for example. Voter registration requirements have long been considered by scholars to be one of the greatest obstacles to voting in elections.[30] In fact, the United States is one of the few developed democracies in the world that requires voters to register to vote; in many countries, registration is automatic when citizens become eligible.

In 1993, President Bill Clinton signed into law the National Voter Registration Act (NVRA, also called the Motor Voter Law), which was designed to make it easier to register to vote (thereby reducing the costs of registering and, by extension, voting) by requiring states to provide voter registration opportunities when individuals apply for (or renew) their driver's licenses or for public assistance or permit Election Day registration. Implementation of the NVRA has varied considerably across states, and evidence that registration or turnout rates have improved significantly since its adoption is elusive.[31] It is conceivable that automatic registration could be more effective. Other approaches to lower costs of voting could be to designate voting to occur on weekends, over multiple days, or to make Election Day a national holiday. Many other countries adopt approaches along these lines, and there is some evidence that these institutional arrangements exert positive effects on participation.[32]

Table 2.5 Reasons for Not Voting (2012 Presidential Election)

Reason	Percent
Too busy, conflicting schedule	19%
Not interested	16%
Illness or disability	14%
Did not like candidates or campaign issues	13%
Out of town	9%
Registration problems	6%
Forgot to vote	4%
Transportation problems	3%
Inconvenient polling place	3%
Bad weather conditions	1%
Other reason	11%
Don't know/refused	3%

Source: U.S. Census Bureau, Current Population Survey (November 2012).

Ways to Engage Citizens and to Improve Participation

Notwithstanding the encouraging developments in presidential voter turnout in recent cycles, we have now established that levels of citizen engagement in elections and politics in the United States generally tend to be quite low. Even in the most prominent elections, like those held to elect the president of the United States, large slices of the eligible population abstain. We have also provided some evidence that low levels of participation can actually accentuate some of the problems that many citizens find worrisome. Here we list some ideas about how to increase citizen participation in public life. This is not an exhaustive list, but it should get readers thinking about the kinds of things that could be done to improve our system.

- Political science studies have repeatedly shown that the application of social pressure can increase an individual's likelihood of voting.[33] In short, people may vote because of reputational considerations. When the act of voting is observable, people want to be perceived to be good citizens by conforming to social norms (like voting in elections). This psychological mechanism may be one of many that exert powerful effects on voting. Finding ways to mobilize voters by reinforcing voting as a civic or social norm they should not violate may be helpful to stimulating more engagement. This could be done by nonprofits, governments, or other groups.
- Many local elections are held off-cycle from national-level elections for the presidency and Congress. Voter turnout in local elections increases appreciably when elections are held on-cycle. This is a simple change that could get more people involved in local politics. Such changes could be accompanied by campaigns that provide voters with information about local candidates so that they are not simply voting for people because they happen to be at the polling place but also because they are armed with good information about the candidates who are running.
- Elections that are competitive attract more voter interest and participation. Unfortunately, many elections in the United States feature just one candidate or are uncompetitive. This could be improved in a number of ways, including developing programs that help challengers raise campaign money. Challengers often have a difficult time raising as much money as incumbents. A number of states, including Maine and Arizona, have adopted clean elections programs that have increased competition in state legislative elections by helping challengers increase their campaign funds.[34]
- Less restrictive ballot access laws (discussed further in Chapter 5) could potentially increase participation and thereby raise the level of electoral competition. In some states, it is quite difficult for parties and candidates with limited resources to get on the ballot. Making it easier for candidates and parties to join the race could make elections more competitive as well as more interesting.
- Political science studies have demonstrated that states that have Election Day registration see higher levels of voter turnout than those that require voters to be registered well in advance. Many states do not have Election Day registration. This change would not

be difficult to implement and would likely increase turnout across states.[35] Other forms of convenience voting (e.g., vote by mail or polling locations in high-traffic locations like malls) as well as automatic registration may have similar effects.

- Political science studies have indicated that social incentives may compel people to participate in public life. One study investigated whether Election Day festivals held at polling places, which featured free snacks, drinks, and music, increase voter turnout. That study found that such festivals increase voter turnout by up to 7%.[36] This is something that could be done by cities or nonprofits to enhance social elements of the voting experience and to make voting more exciting.

- Studies have routinely documented that early socialization experiences can have enduring effects on political behavior. For instance, people who come from politically active families tend to be much more engaged in political life than others. Given the importance of early experiences, it could be worthwhile to get students to understand the importance of political engagement early on in life. For instance, schools could teach students how to vote at an early age or they could work to create an environment where civic norms are fostered. This could be done through curriculum, student groups, or other mechanisms. Students who come from schools where political involvement is viewed as an obligation appear to be more involved in politics than their counterparts as they move forward in life.[37]

- It could be possible to determine ways to incentivize political participation. The city of Los Angeles, for example, is currently considering using prizes or an Election Day lottery to increase voter turnout. Political science studies have indicated that offering individuals nontrivial incentives to vote (e.g., $20 or a $25 gift card) can substantially increase turnout.[38]

- Efforts could be undertaken to enhance the civic significance of Election Day. In 1998, political scientist Martin Wattenberg wrote that we could "move Election Day to the second Tuesday of November and combine it with Veterans' Day, traditionally celebrated on November 11. This would send a strong signal about the importance our country attaches to voting. And what better way could there be to honor those who fought for democratic rights than for Americans to vote on what could become known as Veterans' Democracy Day?"[39] Although we tend to think of Election Day as fixed, it is possible to change the timing of elections if we think it might have a positive effect on citizen engagement.

- Some states are considering imposing fines on people who do not vote. Another idea would be to give people a tax deduction for voting. The state legislature in Hawaii is currently considering a bill that would fine people $100 for not voting.[40] The objection to this idea is, of course, that requiring all people to vote might lead some people to vote without doing any research. It is possible, though, to make changes that increase voter turnout while simultaneously increasing the amount of political information available to voters. For instance, states could devote resources to civic education campaigns.

- One radical change would be to implement mandatory voting. This is something that is used in other countries across the globe. As Martin Wattenberg has noted, "If in an ideal democracy everyone votes, people could simply be required to participate. This is how Australians reasoned when they instituted compulsory voting after their turnout rate fell to 58 percent in 1922. Since then the turnout in Australia has never fallen below 90 percent, even though the maximum fine for not voting is only about $30, and judges readily accept any reasonable excuse."[41] The obvious concern with mandatory voting is that it might be perceived as a violation of individual freedom. However, as political scientist Arend Ljiphart has pointed out, mandatory voting is much less of an imposition than many other legal obligations including jury duty, taxes of all kinds, military service, and compulsory school attendance. He concluded that "before we put the right not to vote on too high a pedestal, let us also remember that non-voting is a form of free riding—taking advantage of the benefits of democracy without contributing to it—and that free riding of any kind may be rational, but that it is also selfish and immoral."[42]

Readers may not like all of these ideas, which is completely reasonable. Our point was not to come up with a list of proposals that would be exhaustive or acceptable to everyone, but instead to point out that there are changes that could be made to potentially improve levels of political engagement in the United States. If political participation is something that we value, it is worth the effort to try to make improvements.

Notes

1. http://newsok.com/only-five-people-vote-in-980000-school-bond-election-in-crutcho/article/3904368.
2. http://blog.sfgate.com/nov05election/2014/06/06/rohnert-park-polling-place-draws-zero-voters/.

3. http://nypost.com/2013/11/06/election-day-turnout-lowest-in-over-50-years/.
4. http://www.ia-sb.org/assets/0f2b4365682d4ae6b538dea1e949b90b.pdf.
5. http://www.rovac.org/documents/Why%20do%20You%20love%20Elections.pdf.
6. http://www.civiced.org/pdfs/books/ElementsOfDemocracy/Elements_Subsection3.pdf.
7. Matthew Streb. 2011. *Rethinking American Electoral Democracy, 2nd Edition.*
8. http://elections.gmu.edu/Turnout_2012G.html.
9. Rosenstone, Steven and John Hansen. 1993. *Mobilization, Participation, and Democracy in America.* New York, NY: Macmillan. Francia, Peter, and Costas Panagopoulos. 2009. "Grassroots Mobilization in the 2008 Presidential Election." *Journal of Political Marketing* 8 (4): 315–333.
10. Goldstein, Kenneth and Travis Ridout. 2002. "The Politics of Participation." *Political Behavior* 24: 3–29.
11. Green, Donald and Alan Gerber. 2008 *Get Out the Vote!* 2nd ed. Washington, DC: Brookings.
12. Panagopoulos, Costas. 2011. "Thank You for Voting: Gratitude Expression and Voter Mobilization." *Journal of Politics* 73 (3): 707–717.
13. http://www.gallup.com/poll/164663/americans-trust-government-generally-down-year.aspx.
14. http://prq.sagepub.com/content/67/1/42.short.
15. http://www.washingtontimes.com/blog/inside-politics/2012/oct/11/turnout-2012-statewide-primaries-lowest-record/.
16. http://fivethirtyeight.blogs.nytimes.com/2010/09/14/primary-voter-turnout-stays-low-but-more-so-for-democrats/?_php=true&_type=blogs&_r=0.
17. http://www.politico.com/story/2014/07/study-record-low-turnouts-seen-in-some-primaries-109221.html.
18. http://www.idea.int/publications/vt/upload/Voter%20turnout.pdf.
19. http://link.springer.com/article/10.1007%2Fs11109-008-9058-9.
20. http://electionstudies.org/nesguide/gd-index.htm#6.
21. http://press.princeton.edu/titles/9685.html.
22. See: http://www.apsanet.org/Files/Memos/voicememo.pdf or http://badattitudes.com/MT/economic.pdf.
23. http://www.pollingreport.com/institut.htm.
24. http://journals.cambridge.org/action/displayFulltext?type=1&fid=8274522&jid=JOP&volumeId=73&issueId=02&aid=8274520.
25. http://faculty.ucmerced.edu/jtrounstine/low_turnout_UAR_RR.pdf.
26. http://onlinelibrary.wiley.com/doi/10.1111/j.1468-2508.2005.00327.x/abstract.
27. http://www.nbcnews.com/news/other/year-low-turnout-consequences-not-voting-f6C10920201.
28. Riker, William and Peter Ordeshook. 1968. "A Theory of the Calculus of Voting." *American Political Science Review* 62(1): 25–42.
29. Brady, Henry E., Sidney Verba and Kay Lehman Schlozman. 1995. "Beyond SES: A Resource Model of Political Participation." *American Political Science Review* 89(2): 271–294.
30. Robert S. Erikson. 1981. "Why Do People Vote? Because They Are Registered." *American Politics Quarterly,* 8: July: 259–276.
31. Highton, Benjamin. 2004. "Voter Registration and Turnout in the United States." *Perspectives on Politics* 2: 507–515.

32. LeDuc, Lawrence, Richard G. Niemi, and Pippa Norris, eds., 2002. *Comparing Democracies 2: New Challenges in the Study of Elections and Voting*. Thousand Oaks, CA: Sage.

33. Panagopoulos, Costas. 2013. "Positive Social Pressure and Prosocial Motivation: Evidence from a Large-Scale Field Experiment on Voter Mobilization." *Political Psychology* 34: 265–275.

34. Malhotra, Neil. 2007. "The Impact of Public Financing on Electoral Competition: Evidence from Arizona and Maine." *State Politics and Policy Quarterly* 8: 263–281.

35. Brians, Craig, and Bernard Grofman. 2001. "Election Day Registration's Effect on U.S. Voter Turnout." *Social Science Quarterly* 82: 170–183.

36. Addonizo, Elizabeth, Donald Green, and James Glaser. 2007. "Putting the Party Back into Politics: An Experiment Testing Whether Election Day Festivals Increase Voter Turnout." *PS: Politics and Political Science* October: 721–727.

37. http://media.hoover.org/sites/default/files/documents/ednext20053unabridged_campbell.pdf.

38. See Panagopoulos, Costas. 2013. "Extrinsic Rewards, Intrinsic Motivation and Voting." *Journal of Politics* 75: 266–280 and http://themonkeycage.org/2012/11/06/incentivizing-participation-would-increase-voter-turnout-and-political-information/.

39. http://www.theatlantic.com/magazine/archive/1998/10/should-election-day-be-a-holiday/305082/.

40. http://www.kitv.com/news/lawmakers-look-at-a-fine-for-those-who-dont-vote/31143276.

41. http://www.theatlantic.com/magazine/archive/1998/10/should-election-day-be-a-holiday/305082/.

42. http://aei.pitt.edu/32418/1/1208943660_pw_54.pdf.

3

MONEY AND SPECIAL
INTERESTS IN ELECTIONS

Jesse Unruh, the former speaker of the California State Assembly, famously described money as "the mother's milk of politics." Former Senator Mark Hanna proclaimed, "There are two things that are important in politics. The first is money and I can't remember what the second one is." Indeed, it is widely believed that money feeds politics and influences how the political system works. While money has long played an important role in campaign politics, the high levels of campaign spending that have been observed in recent election cycles have garnered much scrutiny and fostered much debate. The 2012 presidential election set a record for the highest level of campaign spending in a presidential contest. According to data compiled by the Center for Responsive Politics, spending by the two presidential candidates alone topped $2 billion.[1] That number doesn't even include the money spent by political parties and other groups. If one includes this outside money, approximately $7 billion was spent during the 2012 election.[2] That is a huge sum of money for just one election (the $7 billion doesn't include the amount spent on the 435 House elections and 33 Senate elections in 2012). Such high levels of spending naturally led many people to ask what kinds of public goods or services that money could have bought instead—with answers ranging from lowering poverty to improving public education. Nonetheless, modern campaigns have become remarkably expensive and there is no sign that the costs of campaigns will decrease anytime soon.

In this chapter, we provide a look at levels of campaign spending in national elections, by political candidates as well as by outside groups and interests. The amount of money being funneled into elections by outside groups and parties has been growing over time and has caused great concern among many political observers. We describe the different types of groups that attempt to influence politics by donating to candidates and spending money during elections. Next, we outline some of the concerns that have been raised about money in politics. We focus specifically on the notions that money can "buy" the votes of elected officials and that the money spent on campaigns has no impact on election outcomes—that it is essentially wasted. We also discuss campaign finance reforms that have been implemented to deal with some of the issues surrounding money and elections. In addition, we comment on some of the benefits that come from campaign spending. Despite the negative views that people have about money and politics, decades' worth of research have indicated that high levels of campaign spending correspond to high levels of citizen engagement in politics. The ills of money in politics must be balanced against the benefits. In the end, we provide a discussion of improvements that could be made to campaign finance in the United States.

Campaign Spending in U.S. Elections

Before we discuss the different kinds of actors who attempt to influence politics by donating and spending money during elections, it is worthwhile to take a look at just how much money has been spent in recent races. Figure 3.1 presents data on the total amount of spending in presidential and congressional elections since 1998 (the total reflects the amount of money spent in all congressional races in a given year). These totals reflect money from several sources in addition to the specific campaigns of each candidate. The numbers for presidential spending include money spent by outside groups to fund ads targeting a presidential candidate. The data also include the cost of the conventions and activity by the Democratic National Committee and the Republican National Committee. Congressional spending information includes spending by the candidates, party committees, and 527 groups (tax-exempt groups that do not expressly advocate for the election or defeat of candidates but that spend money on issue advocacy and voter mobilization), including money spent on issue ads and other campaign communications. In general, levels of spending have increased over time. In 1998, the total amount of money spent on congressional elections was $1.6 billion and in 2012 the total rose to $3.6 billion. In the 2000 presidential election, total spending was $1.4 billion and in 2012 it increased to $2.6 billion.

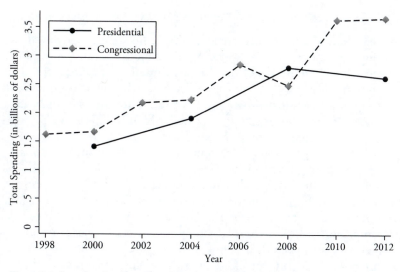

Figure 3.1 Spending Levels in Presidential and Congressional Elections, 1998–2012. Data from https://www.opensecrets.org.

It is worth noting that Americans appear to be concerned about money in politics. A 2012 ABC News/*Washington Post* poll, for instance, showed that 75% of Americans were very or somewhat concerned about the amount of money being spent on political campaign advertising by companies, unions, and wealthy individuals.[3] Americans also appear to be in favor of making changes to the ways that campaigns are financed. In a 2013 Gallup poll, for instance, 50% of people said that they would personally vote for a law establishing a new campaign finance system where federal campaigns are funded by the government and all contributions from individuals and private groups would be banned.[4] In addition, that same poll indicated that 79% of Americans would vote for a law that would put a limit on the amount of money that candidates for the U.S. House and Senate could raise and spend on their political campaigns. Of course, politicians have obvious reasons not to change the rules surrounding campaign finance—many of them benefit from the current levels of campaign spending and see money as important to reelection. Although the campaign finance system has experienced some reforms over time, many people believe that there are still important concerns with the current system. We will discuss some of the main concerns in a section that follows.

Who Raises, Donates, and Spends Money During Elections?

We have already mentioned some of the actors who are involved in making donations and in spending that money during elections. However, a bit more detail on the large number of actors who are involved in the process may be useful. The most obvious actors involved are the political candidates themselves, who are quite interested in raising campaign money. In general, greater dollar figures during fundraising correspond to higher vote shares on Election Day. Candidates often work hard to collect money from donors but in some cases they donate money to their own campaigns. There is no limit to how much of their own money politicians can donate to their campaigns. One interesting trend worth noting is that the composition of Congress has changed significantly over time. Because of the large sums of money needed to campaign (and the unlimited amounts that candidates can donate to their own campaigns), it is not surprising that wealthy individuals are more likely to run for office than those who are not as well off. According to a recent analysis of the wealth of members of Congress, the majority (50.8%) of members of Congress are millionaires.[5] In the House, the median net worth is about $850,000 and in the Senate the median net worth is about $2.8 million.[6]

Ordinary citizens can also donate money to political campaigns, although we should note that only a small portion of the population engages in this political activity (13% reported donating to a party or campaign in 2008).[7] As of the 2013–2014 election season, campaign finance laws limited the amount an individual could give to each candidate (or candidate committee) per election to $2,600. Individuals can donate $32,400 to a national party committee per calendar year; $10,000 to a state, district, or local committee per calendar year; and $5,000 to any other political committee per calendar year. It is interesting to note that until 2014 there was an aggregate limit on how much individuals could give to all of these political groups in total ($123,000 over a two-year election cycle). In a case decided in 2014, *McCutcheon v. Federal Election Commission,* the U.S. Supreme Court ruled that the aggregate limit on campaign donations was unconstitutional under the First Amendment, which guarantees free speech. The logic here was that limiting the number of candidates to whom individuals could give money was a restriction on the ability to express their political preferences. According to the ruling, donors can give to as many candidates and committees as they would like, but they still need to follow the per-candidate, per-PAC, and per–party committee limits.

The restriction on per-candidate, per-PAC, and per–party committee contribution limits is important. One misperception that seems to be pervasive when it comes to money and politics is that individuals can simply write unlimited checks to politicians and campaigns. Although individuals can give to a large number of candidates and campaigns, they must still follow federal and state contribution limits. One interesting development that has garnered attention in recent years is the number of "small" donations (typically, donations under $200) that candidates have collected from individuals. Although most candidates get large campaign donations (greater than $200) from individuals or groups such as PACs, the idea of getting money from donors who give small amounts of money attracts a great deal of positive attention for candidates. Small donations from many different citizens may create the perception that campaigns are democratic and that candidates are not beholden to wealthy individuals. Despite the attention that small donors get during elections, Figure 3.2 illustrates that only a small fraction of candidate campaign money actually comes from small donors. Indeed, during the 2010 election cycle, congressional candidates got just 13% of their overall campaign dollars from small donations (those less than $200). And in recent presidential elections, small donations have accounted for just a small share of the overall money raised by candidates. According to an analysis based on data from the Campaign Finance Institute, "In 2012, President Obama raised only 28% of his campaign funds from donors who gave less than $200 overall, and Romney raised merely 12% from those donors. Both candidates got more of their money from donors giving at least $1,000—in Romney's case, much more. Obama got 39% of his funds from those donors, and Romney got 66%."[8]

Before we move on to a discussion of other actors who are involved in campaign finance, we would like to point out that individuals who donate money to politics tend to be more ideologically extreme than the public at large. Moderates tend to be underrepresented among donors, while extreme liberals and conservatives tend to be overrepresented.[9] Donors also tend to be disproportionately male, white, wealthy, and highly educated.[10] The number of people who donate large sums of money to candidates is also quite small. In 2010, for example, only 0.26% of Americans donated more than $200 to congressional campaigns.[11] But these individuals provided over two-thirds of the total donations. The concern with having a small group of people (who are not representative of ordinary Americans) play a key role in campaign financing is quite clear. If politicians are more responsive to the people who donate to their campaigns than those who do not, then policies and decisions we get out of government may be skewed toward the interests and preferences of donors. Thus, the way that campaigns are funded has serious implications for the process of political representation. Given the importance placed on equity in the United States, it is easy to see why so many people have expressed concern about the role of campaign donors in the political process.

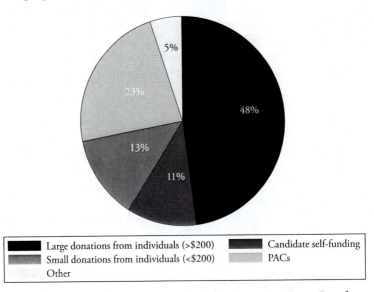

Figure 3.2 Sources of 2010 Congressional Candidate Campaign Money. Data from https://www.opensecrets.org.

In addition to the money donated by candidates and individual citizens, political action committees (PACs) also play a role in campaign financing. A PAC is an organization that is formed to raise and spend money to help elect or defeat political candidates. As we noted above, individuals can donate both to candidates and to PACs. These PACs can then donate money to candidates, following the same limits as individual donors. Most PACs represent particular ideologies, business interests, or labor unions. We should note, though, that political candidates can also create what are called Leadership PACs to help fund the campaigns of other candidates they support. As Figure 3.2 demonstrates, about 23% of congressional campaign money came from PACs during the 2010 elections. Over time, the number of PACs has increased. The Federal Election Commission (FEC) has indicated that from 1974 to 2011 the number of PACs grew from 608 to 4,657.[12] The amount of political contributions made by PACs has also steadily increased over time. One interesting element of how PACs are allowed to operate is their independent expenditures in support of candidates. The term "independent expenditures" is used because federal election law stipulates that expenditures must be made without the participation of the candidates. In other words, in addition to giving money directly to the candidate's campaign, they can fund television ads or other campaign communications that support the candidate (or attack his or her rivals) as *long as they do not coordinate with the candidate directly*.[13]

Over the past several years, the term "Super PAC" has received a great deal of attention. These groups are also known as "independent expenditure-only committees." During recent elections, the media have devoted much attention to Super PACs and their potential influence on politics. Super PACs were created in 2010 after the U.S. Court of Appeals decision in *SpeechNow.org v. FEC*. These new types of PACs do not contribute money to candidates or parties. Instead, they make independent expenditures in federal elections. This means that they can run ads, send mail, or communicate in other ways that advocate for the election or defeat of a candidate. Importantly, there are *no limits or restrictions on the sources of funds* that may be used for the independent expenditures that Super PACs want to make. Thus, these groups can essentially raise unlimited amounts of money from corporations, unions, and individuals and then use that money to advocate for or against political candidates. Federal election law does require that Super PACs report their donors to the Federal Election Commission, although this stipulation hasn't appeared to influence the amounts of money being funneled into national politics. Some Super PACs have found clever ways of getting around the disclosure requirement by channeling money to other organizations before spending it. One thing that differentiates PACs from Super PACs is that Super PACs can't donate money directly to political candidates (PACs are able to do this), although they can use the money they raise to advocate for candidates (there just can't be coordination with the candidates). It is also worth noting that Super PACs can't coordinate with one another, although there is a fine line.

Political candidates and their campaigns often send signals about strategies that outside groups and interests may pick up on. Thus, although groups cannot formally coordinate, they may pursue similar strategies. Indeed, political science studies have shown that in presidential elections, there is a high correlation among the spending patterns of candidates, parties, and outside groups, which signals that groups tend to pursue the same goals and allocate resources in similar ways.[14] It is interesting to note that there is now a large number of Super PACs (1,276 as of 2014). Just the largest 225 of those groups spent a total of $344 million in 2014.[15] It seems likely that the amount spent by Super PACs will increase in upcoming elections.

Another recent court case that has reshaped the campaign finance landscape is *Citizens United v. Federal Election Commission*. In January 2010, the U.S. Supreme Court ruled in *Citizens United* that corporations and unions could fund independent expenditures with money from their general treasuries. Before this ruling, only PACs could make independent expenditures. Since the *Citizens United* case, many corporations and unions are now spending directly from their treasuries. This means that huge sums of money are being spent during federal elections, and it seems likely that this trend will continue into the future. Figure 3.3 provides a look at the amounts of money funding independent expenditures over time. In 2010, the total was $205 million. In 2012, a presidential election year, that number increased to $1 billion. And in 2014, a midterm year, the amount of money spent by outside groups on independent expenditures was $549 million. If you add the figures from just those three election cycles, the total spent on independent expenditures was close to $1.8 billion!

Given the heightened attention to Super PACs in recent years, polling organizations have sought to learn what ordinary Americans think about these organizations. A *Washington Post*/ABC News poll conducted in March 2012 found that Americans are not particularly happy with Super PACs, with 68% responding that Super PACs should be illegal.[16] Americans have long held negative assessments about the role of money in politics, so it is not all that surprising that Super PACs, which pump millions of dollars into elections, are not held in high regard. Another poll, conducted in April 2012, found that 69% of respondents agreed that "new rules that let corporations, unions and people give unlimited money to Super PACs will lead to corruption." Interestingly, 74% of Republicans and 73% of Democrats agreed with this statement, so there is not much of a partisan divide on this issue. In that same poll, 73% of respondents agreed that "there would be less corruption if there were limits on how much could be given to Super PACs." In this case, 75% of Republicans and 78% of Democrats agreed with this statement.[17] Again, there seems to be agreement across party lines about Super PACs and the potential harm they might have on the political system.

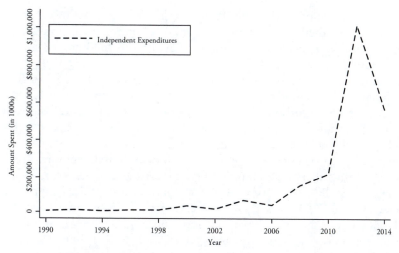

Figure 3.3 Outside Spending over Time in Recent U.S. Election Cycles, 1990–2014. Data from https://www.opensecrets.org.

In addition to the actors mentioned above, 527 groups also play a role in campaign financing. The term "527 group" comes from a section of the U.S. tax code that provides nonprofit status to groups that organize to influence an issue or policy. One of the interesting features of 527 groups is that they can raise unlimited funds from individuals, corporations, or labor unions. The only stipulation is that they are required to register with the IRS and disclose their contributions and expenditures. The activities of 527s explicitly may *not* instruct people to vote for or against a specific candidate, but such groups often will try to influence public opinion about candidates by discussing particular political issues that they think are important. Thus, while 527s cannot advocate for specific candidates or coordinate with candidates, they can engage in "issue advocacy," that is, draw attention to an issue and advocate that voters respond in a certain way come Election Day. They may also engage in voter mobilization efforts. According to OpenSecrets.org, in 2014 there were 210 of these groups and they spent $101 million during the 2014 election cycle.[18]

Political parties also play an important role in campaign finance. Not surprisingly, given their focus on winning elections, political parties raise and spend hundreds of millions of dollars during elections. Political parties are required to collect money only from individuals or PACs. During the 2014 election cycle, the two major parties raised enormous sums: $838 million for the Democrats and $647 million for the Republicans.[19] It is worth noting that each party has committees set up that engage in fundraising. For example, the Democratic National Committee raised $166 million during 2014 and spent $159 million. The Republican National Committee raised $188 million and spent $188 million during 2014.

Interest groups also have a stake in electoral politics. In order to get what they want out of government, interest groups need to have allies. Thus, it's not surprising that interest groups raise and spend money during elections in hopes of getting their preferred candidates elected. There are literally thousands of interest groups in the United States and many of them are involved in electoral politics in a number of ways. It is worth noting that although interest groups can't give money directly to political candidates, they are allowed to contribute via PACs (just to be clear, not all PACs are created by interest groups). As we noted above, PACs use the money they collect from contributions to try to influence elections. Of course, money is not the only way of trying to exert influence. Interest groups can also try to shape public opinion, mobilize voters, endorse candidates, and provide information to potential voters. All of these things can impact elections as well.

What Does Campaign Money Buy?

One question that many people have about the role of money in elections is *What does the money buy?* Campaigns, parties, and outside groups spend money on all kinds of things designed to influence the election outcome, including mailings, get-out-the-vote efforts, billboards, yard signs, campaign managers and staffers, campaign field offices, and other campaign materials. But the core of campaign expenditures is television. On average, modern political campaigns focus about 75% of their spending on television ads.[20] Given the large population of the United States, it makes sense that if candidates want to reach potential voters, they need to do so using the type of media that attracts the most people. Perhaps unsurprisingly, the cost of television advertising has increased over time, meaning that campaigns and groups have to raise large amounts of money in order to be able to advertise using that medium.[21] During the 2012 presidential election, the Obama and Romney campaigns and outside groups ran more than 1 million television advertisements, a record number for any presidential election.[22] According to a report by *The Washington Post*, $404 million was spent on ads supporting Barack Obama and $492 million on ads supporting Mitt Romney.[23]

Although these levels of spending may seem excessive, it is important to note that without it candidates would be hard-pressed to provide the electorate with information. One common criticism is that campaign money is essentially wasted—that it doesn't really have an impact on the electorate or on election outcomes. One news headline after the 2014 election read: "What Americans Could Have Bought Instead of a $4 Billion Election."[24] Although the American public currently seems to have negative perceptions about money in politics, dozens of studies in political science have illustrated that campaign spending is positively related to political engagement.[25] That is, the more money that is spent during elections, the higher voter turnout tends to be. Although people may get tired of hearing about politics and seeing campaign ads during election times, the information provided by campaigns and other groups does a number of important things for the electorate. For one thing, campaign activities tell people that there is an election going on. Most people do not follow politics closely and may be unaware that an election is even happening—this is especially likely for low-salience elections, such as those for state or local offices. In addition, campaign activities provide voters with information about the candidates and issues at stake. Again, Americans tend to be ill-informed about politics and campaign materials can provide some basic political information (e.g., partisan attachments of candidates, issues that are important, contrasts between candidates, etc.). Intense campaigning can also provide voters with a sense that the election is likely to be competitive. When candidates spend large sums of money, it is a signal that the election is important and that there is real competition between those running. Studies have repeatedly shown that more competitive elections (those where the outcome is close) tend to draw more voters to the polls.[26]

In addition to thinking that campaign spending doesn't have an impact on the electorate, many people seem to think that the money *does* have an impact on politicians, fostering corruption. Perhaps the most troubling idea for many people is that campaign donations are essentially "buying" the votes of elected officials. The logic behind this idea is straightforward: If people are giving money (sometimes large amounts) to political candidates, they are going to expect something from them if they get elected. It is clear that the public senses a connection between campaign money and the behavior of those elected to government. One poll asked a sample of Americans the following question: "How much impact do you think big contributions to political parties have on decisions made by the federal government in Washington, D.C?" A staggering 78% of people said that contributions have a "great deal" or "some" impact. In that same poll, 68% of respondents said that "big contributors to political parties sometimes block decisions by the federal government ... that could improve people's everyday lives." Interestingly, 84% of people agreed with the statement that "Members of Congress will be more likely to listen to those who give money to their political party in response to solicitations for large donations." And when asked the following question: "If an individual, issue group, corporation, or labor union donated 50,000 dollars or more to the political party of a Member of Congress, how likely would a Member of Congress be to give the contributor's opinion special consideration because of the contribution?" The poll results showed 82% of people said that the Member of Congress would be "very" or "somewhat" likely to give special consideration.[27]

So do campaign donations to political candidates really "buy" their votes? Political scientists have long been interested in this question—for obvious reasons. If people or groups can simply "buy" the votes of politicians, democracy would be severely undermined. Overall, political scientists have had a difficult time determining whether campaign contributions to elected officials actually buy votes. There is very little conclusive evidence that vote buying occurs systematically. As one study points out, it is difficult to demonstrate that campaign donations *cause* elected officials to vote in certain ways because "donors tend to give to members who are sympathetic to their policy position."[28] Thus, what looks like "vote buying" might just be strategic behavior on the part of those making campaign donations. If individuals or groups give money to a politician who is already likely to support the position they prefer, it's hard to say that the individuals or groups really "bought" the vote.

Another political science study raised an interesting question about campaign contributions and politics: "Why is there so *little* money in American politics?" The authors noticed an interesting puzzle regarding campaign contributions and vote buying: "The discrepancy between the value of policy and the amounts contributed strains basic economic intuitions."[29] For one thing, since certain policy outcomes can be quite valuable to firms and interest groups (e.g., tax breaks, fewer or less stringent regulations, subsidies, etc.), we should see these entities giving more money to elected officials. In addition, the "exceptionally high average rates of return, if real, imply that more firms and industries should enter the political marketplace."[30] In the end, the authors found little relationship between campaign contributions and congressional votes. It appears that donating money to politicians is not a form of policy buying, but is instead an act of political participation and consumption.[31]

Despite the limited political science evidence that vote buying occurs regularly, the *perception* that money from special interests or wealthy individuals influences the votes of elected officials seems to be quite problematic, especially if it diminishes confidence in the system of government or leads people to disengage from politics. One thing worth noting about money and influence is that despite the lack of evidence suggesting that vote buying happens regularly in government, there are certainly other ways that campaign contributions could influence the behavior of elected officials. For example, donors might care not just how a politician votes but also about the wording of a particular section of a policy or about stopping a policy from moving forward. Contributions could also help groups and individuals increase their odds of getting access to a politician if that person is elected to office. It is difficult to measure how much contributions influence these behaviors, but it is certainly possible that contributions influence different elements of the political process besides the votes that are cast by elected officials. Again, if the general public believes that there are inequities in political access or that money has corrosive effects on elected officials, it may be important to consider how to improve the system or perceptions of the system.

It is also worth pointing out that one of the concerns about money in politics is the sheer amount of time members of Congress spend on fundraising. It is really quite shocking how much of their day is devoted to this (approximately four hours per day, according to a recent report, although some have suggested that it is actually more than that).[32] Interestingly, members of Congress think that they will lose the office if they do not spend a great deal of time fundraising and are instructed by party leaders to devote a significant amount of attention to this endeavor. Thus, even though there are many other important things that members of Congress could be doing (e.g., exercising oversight, assisting constituents, researching issues, developing policy alternatives, meeting with those interested in different policy issues, etc.), it appears that fundraising occupies (and will likely continue to occupy) a large chunk of their time.

Campaign Finance Laws and Reforms

Although campaign finance reform is often not an issue at the top of the political agenda due to the perceived importance of issues like the economy, there have been some reforms over time. Before discussing one of the most important national reforms, we should point out that campaign finance regulations and reforms are quite complicated because there are multiple layers of regulations and there is tremendous variation across jurisdictions. For example, in some states, there are virtually no campaign restrictions, individual contribution limits, or limits on corporate or union spending. In the state of Alabama, for example, there are no limits on how much individuals, state parties, PACs, corporations, and unions can give to candidates for state-level offices.[33] Rather than describe all of the different state and local regulations that exist, we prefer to focus on a notable reform passed in 2002—the Bipartisan Campaign Reform Act (BCRA, pronounced *bic-rah*). This act was an attempt to end the use of "soft money" (money raised outside of the limits of campaign finance regulations) in federal elections and to regulate issue advocacy. In addition, BCRA prohibited unions and corporations from spending directly from their treasury funds on electioneering communications—that is, ads that reference a federal candidate and are run within 30 days of a primary election or within 60 days of a general election. Basically, the law said that if unions or corporations wanted to broadcast ads about a candidate, they had to sponsor a PAC to buy the ads.

Although BCRA attracted a great deal of attention, it is important to note that its impact was altered by a series of rulings by the Supreme Court. In a 2003 case, *McConnell v. FEC,* the Court upheld the constitutionality of most of BCRA (the control of soft money and regulation of electioneering) but struck down two elements of the act. First, the Supreme Court ruled against a section of BCRA stipulating that a party committee was not allowed to make both coordinated (that is, in collaboration with candidates) and independent expenditures (described above) on behalf of a candidate after that candidate's general election nomination. Under BCRA, a party committee was required to decide—when a candidate was nominated—if it was going to help the candidate through either limited coordinated expenditures or unlimited independent expenditures. Under the *McConnell* ruling, it is possible for party committees to engage in both types of spending after a candidate is nominated. The Supreme Court also overturned the prohibition against political contributions by minors (defined as persons 17 and younger in BCRA). The *Citizens United* case mentioned above also has implications for BCRA. *Citizens United* struck down the provision in BCRA that limited the amount of money that corporations and unions could spend, which means that these entities can now spend unlimited funds directly on independent expenditures. Just to be clear, most of BCRA is still the law of the land, but the *Citizens United* ruling has made it easier for corporations and unions to get involved in politics because they can now spend money directly from their own treasuries—something that BCRA was trying to limit. As we noted above, many corporations and unions have already taken advantage of this newfound ability and we are seeing large sums of money being spent during federal elections.

Although BCRA represents one reform, we should point out that many states and localities across the United States have attempted to improve campaign finance. As of 2013, 25 states have developed programs that provide public funds during elections.[34] Public funding entails using government money to help pay for campaign expenses. Such programs typically either provide funds to individual candidates or to political parties. In some cases, state programs provide tax incentives to individuals who make campaign contributions. Some states combine a number of these approaches. A number of municipalities across the United States, including some of the largest cities like New York City and Los Angeles, have also implemented public funding programs.[35] A brief description of one city's approach to public finance may help illuminate how such approaches work. In Albuquerque, New Mexico, voters approved the Open and Ethical Elections Program in 2005, which provides public campaign funding to qualifying candidates. Essentially what this does is allocate a certain amount of public money to a fund that is then used to provide municipal candidates with campaign money. The program is designed to get candidates to focus on the issues that are important to voters rather than to spend a great deal of their time fundraising. It is also supposed to enhance public confidence in the electoral processes, given the concerns that people have about donations buying influence. One interesting feature of the program is that it provides participating candidates with supplemental funds if they are running against a candidate who does not participate in the program and exceeds a certain threshold of campaign spending. This is an effort to ensure that publicly funded elections remain competitive and that the program does not disadvantage participants. We should point out, though, that it can be hard for publicly funded candidates to keep up with their competitors if those competitors are extremely well funded and opt out of public financing programs. During the 2009 New York City mayoral election, for example, Michael Bloomberg, whose campaign was self-funded, ran against and beat Bill Thompson, who accepted public financing. Bloomberg spent about $110 million and Thompson spent about $10 million, meaning that Bloomberg outspent Thompson by a ratio of 11:1.[36]

In Albuquerque (and in many other places), the public funding program is voluntary (candidates can still choose to fund their campaigns through private contributions), although over 60% of candidates running for municipal elections in Albuquerque have accepted public financing.[37] The program was first used during the 2007 municipal elections, but some reports have suggested that levels of campaign spending have declined since the program has been implemented and that there have been no misuses of funds.[38] One concern with public financing is that the Supreme Court ruled in *Buckley v. Valeo* (1976) that limiting the total amount a candidate can spend was a violation of the First Amendment's guarantee of free speech. The challenge that this case creates for those who support the public financing of campaigns is that not all candidates may opt to participate. This is certainly problematic for those who believe that public financing helps to eliminate some of the problems associated with money in politics. Of course, public financing systems may create new problems altogether. It may disadvantage candidates who opt to participate or limit the amount of resources that campaigns have to disseminate information and communicate with voters. As we mentioned above, candidates often need large amounts of money in order to communicate their message to potential voters, especially when their constituency is large.

Although supporters of reforms like public financing are often displeased with the high levels of campaign spending in elections, there is an alternative perspective: Others believe we should spend even *more* on campaigns than we already do. Elections are crucial to achieving political representation and accountability. Thus, it seems quite important that people engage in elections. Political science studies have demonstrated that one way to get people engaged in electoral politics is to foster a sense of political competition and to provide them with information that mobilizes them.[39] The activities of campaigns, which are funded by campaign donations, play an important role in fostering that competition and providing that political information. The implication is that if we want to increase citizen engagement, we may need to spend even more on campaigns. Each year, U.S. companies spend millions to market paper towels (Procter & Gamble spends about $63 million) and yogurt (General Mills spends about $62 million to advertise Yoplait Light alone) but campaigns typically only spend a few dollars per voter to urge them to vote.[40] Campaign communication is quite expensive, especially when it involves television ads, and it requires a great deal of effort to reach large groups of people (the average size of a congressional district is 700,000 people and the U.S population is about 320 million people). Campaign spending is essential to getting citizens involved in the electoral process. It is interesting to note that there is a huge discrepancy between perceptions of campaign spending levels and actual spending levels in elections. Indeed, studies have indicated that individuals think that U.S. House candidates spend as much as 10 times what they actually do. Given this misperception, it is perhaps unsurprising that people are so concerned about campaign spending levels. Of course, the implication is that with more accurate information, perhaps the public might not be as alarmed by campaign spending as they currently are. Though it may seem contradictory to say that more money should be spent during elections given the concerns that people have about money in elections, it's important to note that the *total* amount of money being spent may not be the problem (and perhaps should be increased). Instead, *where the money comes from* (e.g., wealthy donors that are unrepresentative of ordinary Americans) and *how it is obtained* (e.g., while members of Congress could be working on policy, etc.) may be more concerning. There are, of course, ways of remedying these things and increasing the transparency of the campaign fundraising and spending process.

Before discussing some ways that the campaign finance system could be improved, we should point out that at the federal level, the enforcement of campaign finance regulations has been challenging. The Federal Election Commission is in charge of enforcement, but reports have documented that it is quite understaffed, is facing further staff cuts, and often has a difficult time pursuing complaints in a timely or efficient manner.[41] In addition, there has been partisan debate about the value of the commission. According to a recent report, "Analysts charged with scouring disclosure reports to ensure candidates and political committees are complying with laws have a nearly quarter-million-page backlog."[42] The fact that large sums of money are continually entering into politics and that the key agency in charge of monitoring and enforcement is facing severe limitations makes it difficult to avoid some of the problems and negative perceptions associated with money in elections.

Ways to Improve Campaign Finance

As we did in the previous chapter, we would like to provide some ideas on how campaign finance in the United States could be improved. Again, this is not designed to be an exhaustive list but it should get readers thinking about the kinds of things that could be done to make the system better.

- Ordinary citizens could do a better job of monitoring the campaign activities of political candidates. One of the ideas that often gains traction when it comes to money in politics is that campaign finance is not sufficiently transparent. Many people do not realize that there is already a great deal of information available regarding campaign donations and expenditures. The Federal

Election Commission website, for example, contains a wealth of campaign spending data that interested citizens could use to help inform their decisions about politicians. At the federal level, it is possible to get information on who donates to candidates, how much is donated, and how they spend campaign money—almost in real time. This is also possible in some states and localities. Citizens could start making use of the information that is already (and increasingly) available to them.

- Citizens could press elected officials to increase the resources available to the FEC to administer and enforce election regulations. As we noted above, the FEC has a difficult time addressing complaints because it is short on resources. If people think that there are problems with campaign finance, one way to address those problems is to give the government more resources and authority to investigate concerns.

- Citizens could push government officials to reform the campaign finance system. One of the problems with creating reform is that campaign finance often gets displaced by other issues on the political agenda (e.g., economic performance, health care, etc.). If, through vigorous political participation, citizens demand that policymakers act on this issue and are willing to vote them out of office if they do not, it may be possible to develop new legislation that improves the federal campaign finance system. Recently, a constitutional amendment called the *Democracy for All Amendment*, which would have given Congress and the states the power to set limits on campaign spending, was blocked in the U.S. Senate. If ordinary Americans want to implement campaign limits, they could urge their elected officials to take up this amendment once again. If elected officials do not, voters would need to hold them accountable by voting them out of office.

- It is worth noting that ordinary citizens have the capacity to express their preferences via financial support. One way to offset large campaign donations is to promote campaign financing via small donations. Montgomery County in Maryland is considering offering incentives to encourage ordinary citizens to donate money to candidates. The legislation being considered there provides candidates with a trade-off between declining interest group contributions and accepting public funds. Essentially, if candidates decline special interest contributions, they would become eligible for fairly large amounts of public matching funds. In order to get the funds, candidates would also need to show that they could get some support from constituents in the form of small donations ($150 or less). According to an analysis of how the program works, if a candidate for the county executive position could raise $150,000 by getting 3,000 donations of $50 each, the candidate would then be eligible for $900,000 in public funds.[43] Offering good matching ratios is one potential solution to the problem of candidates not wanting to accept public funding because they can raise huge sums of money when they do not take the public funds. Other places could consider implementing similar programs if they believe that some individuals and groups exert too much pull on political candidates.

- If citizens are concerned about levels of campaign spending and having more transparency, they should monitor government activities to make sure that new policies do not abolish contribution limits or disclosure requirements.

Notes

1. https://www.opensecrets.org/bigpicture/.
2. http://www.politico.com/story/2013/01/7-billion-spent-on-2012-campaign-fec-says-87051.html.
3. http://www.washingtonpost.com/page/2010-2019/WashingtonPost/2012/09/17/National-Politics/Polling/question_6672.xml?uuid=ZaDSNgC3EeK78OM7TuLw6A.
4. http://www.gallup.com/poll/163208/half-support-publicly-financed-federal-campaigns.aspx.
5. http://www.opensecrets.org/news/2015/01/one-member-of-congress-18-american-households-lawmakers-personal-finances-far-from-average/.
6. http://www.opensecrets.org/news/2015/01/one-member-of-congress-18-american-households-lawmakers-personal-finances-far-from-average/.
7. http://electionstudies.org/nesguide/toptable/tab6b_5.htm.
8. http://www.vox.com/2014/7/30/5949581/money-in-politics-charts-explain.
9. Panagopoulos, Costas, and Daniel Bergan. 2006. "Contributions and Contributors in the 2004 Presidential Election Cycle." *Presidential Studies Quarterly* 36: 155–171.
10. Ibid.
11. http://www.vox.com/2014/7/30/5949581/money-in-politics-charts-explain.
12. http://www.manhattan-institute.org/html/lpr_15.htm.
13. The technical definition of an independent expenditure is something "expressly advocating the election or defeat of a clearly identified candidate that is not made in cooperation, consultation, or concert with, or at the request or suggestion of, a candidate, a candidate's authorized committee, or their agents, or a political party or its agents." http://www.fec.gov/pages/brochures/indexp.shtml.
14. Panagopoulos, Costas. 2006. "Vested Interests: Interest Group Resource Allocation in Presidential Campaigns." *Journal of Political Marketing* 5: 59–78.
15. https://www.opensecrets.org/outsidespending/fes_summ.php.

16. http://www.washingtonpost.com/wp-srv/politics/polls/postabcpoll_031012. html.
17. http://www.brennancenter.org/analysis/national-survey-super-pacs-corruption-and-democracy.
18. https://www.opensecrets.org/527s/index.php.
19. https://www.opensecrets.org/parties/.
20. http://wiscadproject.wisc.edu.
21. http://www.unm.edu/~nmpirg/freeair/freeair.html.
22. http://www.washingtonpost.com/blogs/post-politics/wp/2012/11/02/romney-campaign-ads-outnumber-obama-ads-in-final-stretch/.
23. http://www.washingtonpost.com/wp-srv/special/politics/track-presidential-campaign-ads-2012/.
24. http://www.cnn.com/2014/11/01/politics/4-billion-expensive-election/.
25. See Holbrook, Thomas, and Aaron C. Weinschenk. 2014. "Campaigns, Mobilization, and Turnout." *Political Research Quarterly* 67:44–52. See also Hall, Melinda Gann, and Chris Bonneau. 2008. "Mobilizing Interest: The Effects of Money on Citizen Participation in State Supreme Court Elections." *American Journal of Political Science* 52: 457–470.
26. See Evans, Heather K. 2014. *Competitive Elections and Democracy in America: The Good, the Bad, and the Ugly*. New York, NY: Routledge. See also Holbrook, Thomas, and Aaron C. Weinschenk. 2014. "Campaigns, Mobilization, and Turnout." *Political Research Quarterly* 67: 44–52.
27. Survey results reported in this article: http://scholarship.law.upenn.edu/cgi/viewcontent.cgi?article=1366&context=penn_law_review.
28. http://www.cfinst.org/pdf/papers/02_Powell_Influence.pdf.
29. Ansolabehere, Stephen, John M. de Figueiredo, and James M. Snyder Jr. 2003. "Why Is There So Little Money in U.S. Politics?" *The Journal of Economic Perspectives* 17: 105–130.
30. Ibid.
31. Ibid.
32. See http://www.washingtonpost.com/blogs/wonkblog/wp/2013/01/14/the-most-depressing-graphic-for-members-of-congress/ *and* http://www.theatlantic.com/politics/archive/2013/06/the-humiliating-fundraising-existence-of-a-member-of-congress/277227/.
33. For more information see http://www.ncsl.org/research/elections-and-campaigns/campaign-contribution-limits-overview.aspx and http://www.ncsl.org/Portals/1/documents/legismgt/Limits_to_Candidates_2012-2014.pdf.
34. For a list of state programs, see http://www.ncsl.org/research/elections-and-campaigns/public-financing-of-campaigns-overview.aspx.
35. A full list can be found here: http://users.polisci.wisc.edu/kmayer/466/Keeping_It_Clean.pdf.
36. http://www.nyccfb.info/PDF/per/2009_PER/2009PostElectionReport.pdf.
37. http://www.policyarchive.org/handle/10207/96100.
38. http://www.policyarchive.org/handle/10207/96100.
39. Green, Donald, and Alan Gerber. 2008. *Get Out the Vote: How to Increase Voter Turnout, 2nd Edition*. Brookings.
40. http://www.nytimes.com/2009/10/03/nyregion/03finance.html?_r=0.

41. http://www.washingtonpost.com/blogs/the-fix/wp/2013/12/18/the-most-impor-tant-political-story-you-havent-heard-about/.
42. http://www.washingtonpost.com/blogs/the-fix/wp/2013/12/18/the-most-impor-tant-political-story-you-havent-heard-about/.
43. http://www.washingtonpost.com/opinions/a-montgomery-county-campaign-finance-bill-that-empowers-small-donors/2014/09/13/33fdaac8-3ac7-11e4-8601-97ba88884ffd_story.html.

4

PRESIDENTIAL ELECTIONS

Every four years, U.S. presidential elections generate considerable media attention, excitement, and debate. Even people who aren't normally all that interested in politics often become engaged because of all of the "hoopla" surrounding the election. Campaign advertisements fill the airwaves (at least in some places); candidates crisscross the country making campaign stops in many states; pollsters constantly survey the American electorate to learn which candidate is in the lead; and media outlets report on each candidate's every move. It is hard to avoid politics during presidential election years, especially if one lives in a state that the campaigns view as being "up for grabs." Given the importance of the presidency in the United States, it is not surprising that presidential elections typically attract higher levels of voter participation than congressional midterm, state, or local elections. Despite the prominence of presidential elections, many Americans find some features of our electoral system to be confusing and, at times, frustrating. In this chapter, we focus on three important aspects of the presidential election process—the selection of candidates, the role of the Electoral College, and the factors that influence election outcomes.

The Selection of Presidential Nominees

For many people, the most interesting aspect of presidential elections is the candidate pool. Who are the candidates among whom voters will get to choose? Unlike local elections, which often attract candidates with little experience in politics, presidential elections typically draw candidates who have significant previous experience in government as well as national reputations. In the 2012 election, for example, Barack Obama had previously served as a U.S. senator and Mitt Romney had previously served as the governor of Massachusetts and was the runner-up for the Republican nomination in the previous presidential contest in 2008. As presidential campaigns unfold, most people develop at least some familiarity with the candidates, but many people do not have a clear understanding of how the candidates are selected. In part, this is probably due to the fact that the selection process takes place over an extended period of time. Although the presidential nominating conventions are technically the place where the candidates are officially chosen, the selection process begins long before the conventions are held.

Two institutions play a crucial role in selecting candidates in U.S. presidential elections: primaries and caucuses. Primaries are elections held (using secret ballots) before the general election to narrow the pool of candidates. Most states use primary elections. Caucuses are face-to-face gatherings held prior to the general election at local party events where registered partisans vote on the candidates. Typically, voting at caucuses is done by raising hands or breaking up into small groups. The state of Iowa is perhaps best known for its use of caucuses (it also goes first in the sequence of state contests), but other states use this method as well. Interestingly, the caucus system was the original mechanism that parties used to select candidates, but during the early twentieth century, there was a push toward the primary system because people believed that the secret ballot was a better way of making choices. A breakdown of which states use primaries or caucuses is provided in Table 4.1.

In both primaries and caucuses, participants do not technically vote directly for a candidate; instead, their votes determine the number of delegates committed to a specific candidate that will be sent by the state parties to the national conventions held in the summer before the general election. These delegates are expected to vote at the convention for the candidates they have pledged to support, at least in the first round of balloting. The process of voting for delegates rather than the candidates themselves is a remnant of the elitist system of not trusting the citizens. It also allows for a decision on the convention floor in the case of no early winner emerging. If there is a clear leader in the delegate count, this distinction of voting for delegates rather than candidates has no real meaning. But if there is not a leader going into the convention, then delegates may end up shifting their support to another candidate to create a majority winner.

In order to win the party's nomination, then, candidates have to win a series of primaries and caucuses in the states. It is interesting to note that there is considerable variation in who is allowed to participate in caucuses and primaries. Table 4.1 indicates whether states have open, closed, or semi-closed caucuses or primaries. In general, open primaries and caucuses allow voters of any affiliation to vote in the election of any party they select (though they cannot vote in more than one). Interestingly, there are sometimes concerns about "party crashing" or the idea that partisans might strategically vote for a weaker candidate in another party's primary (with the hope being that the opposing party nominates a weak candidate who is easier to defeat in the general election). In a closed primary or caucus, only registered voters within a party can vote in that party's nomination election. Independents are typically not allowed to participate. In a semi-closed primary or caucus, unaffiliated voters get to select in which party contest to vote, while registered voters can vote only in their party's primary or caucus. We should also note that there is variation across parties in terms of who is allowed to participate. For example, in the state of Hawaii, anyone can vote in the Republican caucus as long as they fill out a Republican Party card on that day, but only registered Democrats are allowed to participate in the Democratic caucus. We should also note that the methods for awarding delegates vary by party. The Democratic Party uses a proportional method (candidates receive the percentage of delegates matching their vote share), while the Republican Party allows each state to decide whether to use a proportional or winner-take-all method.

States' selections of either primary or caucus systems are not inconsequential. Due to the nature of each type of election, there are typically big differences in terms of participation rates as well as the demographic and ideological composition of the respective electorates. Caucuses tend to attract fewer and more ideologically extreme voters compared to primaries. Consider that in the 2008 Democratic presidential primary election in Texas, the Lone Star State had both a primary and a caucus on the very same day; Barack Obama won the caucuses, and Hillary Clinton triumphed in the primary. One study found that in 2008 turnout in caucuses was about 22 percentage points lower than it was in primaries.[1] One potential reason for the low participation in caucuses could be the fact that caucuses entail the public expression of preferences while primaries entail using secret ballots. Since many people are averse to publically revealing their preferences, the nature of caucuses may discourage participation. That study also found evidence that the issue preferences of primary voters more closely reflect the overall distribution of preferences in the general population than the issue preferences of caucus participants. In a section that follows, we provide a suggestion for reform that entails moving away from caucuses.

Table 4.1 Presidential Primaries and Caucuses Across the American States in 2012

States with Caucuses	States with Primaries	States with Both
Alaska (O)	Alabama (O)	Missouri (O)
Colorado (C)	Arizona (C)	Nebraska (SC)
Hawaii (Rep O, Dem C)	Arkansas (O)	Utah (Rep C, Dem O)
Idaho (Rep C, Dem SC)	California (Rep C, Dem SC)	
Iowa (C)	Connecticut (C)	
Kansas (C)	Delaware (C)	
Maine (C)	Florida (C)	
Minnesota (O)	Georgia (O)	
Montana (O)	Illinois (SC)	
Nevada (C)	Indiana (O)	
North Dakota (Rep C, Dem O)	Kentucky (C)	
Washington (Rep C, Dem SC)	Louisiana (C)	
Wyoming (C)	Maryland (C)	
	Massachusetts (SC)	
	Michigan (O)	
	Mississippi (O)	
	New Hampshire (SC)	
	New Jersey (C)	
	New Mexico (C)	
	New York (C)	
	North Carolina (SC)	
	Ohio (O)	
	Oklahoma (C)	
	Oregon (C)	
	Pennsylvania (C)	
	Rhode Island (SC)	
	South Carolina (O)	
	South Dakota (Rep C, Dem O)	
	Tennessee (O)	
	Texas (O)	
	Vermont (O)	
	Virginia (O)	
	West Virginia (SC)	
	Wisconsin (O)	

Notes: Data from http://www.fec.gov/pubrec/fe2012/2012pdates.pdf *and* http://www.fairvote. org/research-and-analysis/presidential-elections/congressional-and-presidential-primaries-open-closed-semi-closed-and-top-two/.

O: Open, C: Closed, SC: Semi-closed, Rep C: Closed for the Republican Party, Dem O: Open for the Democratic Party, Rep O: Open for the Republican Party, Dem C: Closed for the Democratic Party, Dem SC: Semi-closed for the Democratic Party.

The timing and sequence of primaries and caucuses is also quite important. For decades, states have attempted to leapfrog over each other to schedule their primaries and caucuses earlier and earlier. This has resulted in a phenomenon called "frontloading." The basic idea is that early primaries and caucuses will have a more pronounced effect on the nominations than later ones. Thus, party leaders have a desire to move their elections to the front of the cycle. The Iowa caucuses and New Hampshire primary hold coveted spots in the sequence of nomination elections with the Iowa caucuses occurring first and the New Hampshire primaries following closely behind. Both states have laws on the books that automatically move their dates forward in response to a change made by any other state, ensuring their primacy in the system. The rest of the states hold their elections in the weeks and months after but still jockey for position against each other in every new election season, so the calendar is never fixed. One day in particular—Super Tuesday (the day when the largest number of states hold their elections)—typically attracts a great deal of attention.

States are increasingly interested in holding their nominating contests as early as possible in order to have some meaningful say in which candidate ultimately emerges victorious. By the time voters in states that vote late in the process cast their primary ballots, a candidate may have already pulled apart from the herd or even amassed enough delegate support to emerge as the presumptive nominee; in such a scenario, votes cast in these states would be largely irrelevant. Typically, candidate attention (effort, time, money) and media attention (coverage) are showered on early-voting states while late-voting states are relegated to relative obscurity. Unsurprisingly, participation in primaries and caucuses that occur late in the process tends to be lower than in states whose contests are held earlier in the process.

Frontloading is an interesting phenomenon that has important political consequences. Indeed, many people have expressed concern that a frontloaded nomination process could make it hard for a candidate who doesn't have momentum early on to win the election. Candidates can capitalize on the momentum culled from early victories in states like Iowa and New Hampshire to do better in subsequent contests in other states. As one political observer noted, "Early losses doom momentum candidates. Front runners, on the other hand, can easily survive the early losses because they already have the resources to continue."[2] Put another way, "frontloading benefits front runners, the two front runners usually become the nominees of the two major parties, and one of the two major party nominees wins the presidential election."[3]

Given the importance of primaries and caucuses, the competition between candidates to win primary and caucus voters (and subsequently delegates) often gets quite intense. For example, the 2012 Republican contest was highly contested and uncertain until Mitt Romney accumulated enough delegates late in the season to displace a long list of competitors. In 2008, Barack Obama and Hillary Clinton (the early front-runner) went almost to the end of the season before Obama gained a majority of delegates, heading off speculation that the final result might be decided at the convention by what are known as superdelegates. (In addition to delegates, the Democratic Party has superdelegates who are not pledged to support any particular candidate—generally superdelegates are state officeholders or people who hold important positions within the party.) To provide a sense of how many delegates participate in the conventions, in the 2008 election Democrats had 3,515 pledged delegates and 852 superdelegates at their convention, and the Republican convention featured 2,488 delegates.[4]

We should point out that even before the primaries and caucuses, candidates interested in running for the presidency are hard at work. Political scientists call the time between when candidates announce their interest in office and when the primaries and caucuses are held the "invisible primary." During the invisible primary, candidates try to raise campaign money, build support, and make speeches to demonstrate that they will be viable contenders. The invisible primary is important because party leaders can play an important role in determining which candidates will be taken seriously and which will not. As one political scientist has pointed out, "by the time the voters get involved, the parties send powerful cues about which candidates are acceptable, and the others either drop out or have little chance."[5] Indeed, research has shown that a candidate's level of party support (from party insiders) has a great deal of influence on his or her chance of getting the nomination.[6]

The selection of presidential candidates is complex. As we noted above, each state has different rules that determine how its nomination election works, who can participate, and when they are held. The process culminates in the national party conventions. The nominating conventions are events that take place over several days in the late summer or early fall (depending on, among other things, the timing of the Olympics and the NFL opening games). In the past, the nominating conventions were places where the candidates would actually be chosen. In modern presidential elections, the question of who will be nominated is now settled before the conventions (caucus participants and primary voters determine who the candidates will be by selecting delegates to represent them at the conventions), although the nominations technically do not become official until the roll call vote at the conventions. Even though presidential nominees are generally known well before the conventions actually occur, the conventions remain important events due to the high levels of media attention they generate for the candidates. They have evolved into well-scripted spectacles designed to get potential voters excited about the candidates as well as to provide information about their personalities and what they will do if elected. We will return to the importance of conventions when we discuss the role of campaigns during presidential elections.

The Electoral College

Another important aspect of presidential elections to consider is the Electoral College, which is perhaps one of the most controversial features of the U.S. presidential election process. The Electoral College is also one of the things that many Americans find to be remarkably frustrating. Gallup has occasionally asked the American public about this facet of our elections and it does not earn high marks. In a 2011 poll, 62% of Americans said that they would amend the U.S. Constitution to employ a popular vote system and just 35% said that they would keep the Electoral College.[7] Interestingly, in every poll that Gallup has conducted since 1967, the majority of Americans have favored a popular vote system.[8]

Although most people have some sense of what the Electoral College is (and whether they like it or not), a quick overview may be helpful. The Electoral College is the institution that elects the president and the vice president (it's not an actual place, but rather a *process* of selection). In the United States, the popular vote does not *directly* decide the winner of presidential elections. Instead, voters in each state actually choose "electors" by casting votes for the presidential candidate of their choice (in some states the electors are actually listed on the ballot below the candidate names and in other states voters just see the presidential candidates listed—even though they are technically voting for electors and not the candidates themselves). Electors are typically selected to recognize service to parties. For instance, electors might be elected officials from the state level (e.g., state legislators) or party leaders (e.g., Democratic Party Chair). In 2008 in Wisconsin, the Democratic candidate won the state and the 10 Democratic electors (Wisconsin has ten electoral votes) that included the governor, a state senator, two state Assembly members, a former state cabinet member, the chair of the state Democratic Party, and four legislative candidates. The electors cast their electoral votes (each elector gets one vote for president and one for vice president) for candidates when the Electoral College meets right after Election Day. Just to be clear, on Election Day voters are not actually voting for the candidates, but instead for *electors who have pledged to support the candidates.* The Electoral College is made up of 538 of these electors (each state gets an elector for each member in the House of Representatives and one for each of its senators; the District of Columbia gets three electors, the minimum number for any state.) The candidates' goal is to win a majority, or at least 270 electoral votes—the minimum number of electoral votes that is required to elect a president. In 48 states (and in Washington, D.C.), the candidate who wins most of the votes in a state wins all of the state's electoral votes. In Maine and Nebraska, electoral votes can be split. In these two states, the top vote getter wins two electoral votes and the remaining votes are awarded to the vote winner in each congressional district (there are two in Maine and three in Nebraska).

If no candidate manages to receive a majority (270) of electoral votes—which is conceivable if there are strong independent or minor-party contenders—the U.S. House of Representatives elects the president from among the top three electoral-vote recipients. Scenarios like this are exceedingly rare, but they have happened. In 1824, for example, no candidate achieved a majority of electoral votes. They were split among Andrew Jackson, from Tennessee (99 votes), John Quincy Adams (84), Secretary of State William Crawford (who suffered a stroke before the election, 41), and Kentucky's Henry Clay (37). Once Clay was eliminated (he came in fourth place), he threw his support behind Adams, who was ultimately elected by the House. When presidential elections wind up in the U.S. House for resolution, each state's congressional delegation is entitled to a single vote. That means large states like California would exert the same degree of influence as tiny states like Delaware or Rhode Island (the District of Columbia would not even get a vote), a situation considered by many to be even less equitable or "democratic" than the Electoral College itself. One reason most states award electoral votes by "winner take all" is to avoid precisely this possibility. Failure to achieve a majority of electoral votes by vice presidential contenders results in the decision being rendered by the U.S. Senate, in which each senator is entitled to one vote to be cast for one of the top-two electoral vote recipients (the Senate has chosen the vice president once in U.S. history, in the 1836 election). Note that each chamber can ultimately make decisions that coincide (or not) with the popular vote and even choose a president and vice president of different parties in such circumstances!

The fact that U.S. presidents are not directly elected has long bothered many Americans. It is also troubling for many that it is possible for a candidate to win the popular vote but not win the Electoral College vote. Indeed, "a misalignment of the popular and electoral vote generally results from one candidate narrowly winning a number of states with a majority of the electoral votes, while losing badly in other states."[9] This has happened four times in U.S. history (in 1824, 1876, 1888, and 2000). In the most recent instance (2000), Republican George W. Bush received 271 electoral votes to become president, despite the fact that Al Gore, the Democratic contender, won the popular vote by more than 500,000 votes nationwide.

One of the questions that many people have about the Electoral College is *Why does it exist?* In order to understand the development of this institution, one needs to consider the perspectives of the Framers of the Constitution. Because many of the Founders feared that a tyrant could manipulate the public and gain power, they created the Electoral College as a way of making sure that it wouldn't be possible to manipulate the citizenry. In short, the Electoral College was a check on the electorate, which could potentially be fooled to support a person who might not be well suited for office or who might be interested in abusing government power. The Founders had a number of fears about the results of a direct popular vote. One of these fears was that states with large populations would always decide the presidency. They thought that the Electoral College would be a way of creating a system of fairness among the states. (It is important to note that the Founders thought in terms of states. It is also worth noting that, without the Electoral College, campaigning would revolve around cities with major populations, which would discriminate against rural voters.) Another fear, rooted in the elitism of the Founders, was that average citizens weren't knowledgeable enough to elect a president without the Electoral College. In short, they didn't want the uneducated and irresponsible masses—who knew little of politics—to select the nation's leader. Many of the Founders were fearful of too much democracy. In Federalist No. 68, Alexander Hamilton wrote that an electoral process should ensure that "the office of President will never fall to the lot of any man who is not in an eminent degree endowed with the requisite qualifications."[10] According to Hamilton, the Electoral College would preserve "the sense of the people," while also making sure that "a small number of persons, selected by their fellow citizens from the general mass, will be most likely to possess the information and discernment requisite to such complicated investigations."[11] In addition, there were concerns that if a direct popular vote was used to select the president, voters might not be able to get information about candidates from outside of their own state. Remember that at this point in time national political campaigns weren't feasible (as they are now) because the population was widely dispersed and a transportation and communication infrastructure was not well developed. Also remember that the Founders didn't anticipate the development of political parties, which provide candidates with a "brand name" to run under—something that simplifies the electoral process for candidates and voters. Of course, we now know that political parties emerged shortly after the founding. The Founders thought that if people only learned about a candidate from their state or region (which seemed likely to them given the lack of parties and the lack of infrastructure to support national campaigning), they would likely vote for that person, which could lead to a situation where the national vote—and the nation—was divided among a number of regional candidates, none of whom could command a majority of the popular vote. The answer to these concerns was the Electoral College system.

It is interesting to note that the Electoral College has shaped the strategic context of presidential elections. As we noted above, presidential elections are often thought of as a "race to 270."[12] Campaigns want to win at least 270 electoral votes and are constantly trying to determine how to win enough states in order to reach the magic number. Virtually all states use a winner-take-all method for awarding electoral votes. (The decision about how to allocate votes is up to each individual state; the Constitution does not mandate the use of the winner-take-all method.) This means that the person who wins a state gets all of that state's electoral votes, regardless of the margin of victory (i.e., a win by a margin of 1% gets a candidate the same result as a win by a margin of 30%). During presidential campaigns, the candidates typically have a good sense of which states are solidly Democratic and which are solidly Republican. Thus, the campaigns tend to focus on the states that are "up for grabs." These states are typically called "battleground" or "swing" states. Candidates do not have much of an incentive to invest in states where they are leading or losing by huge margins, focusing the election on the swing states.

In each election cycle, the number of battleground states is typically quite small. In 2012, for example, Colorado, Florida, Iowa, Nevada, New Hampshire, North Carolina, Ohio, Virginia, and Wisconsin were widely agreed to be the swing states.[13] Given that these states were viewed as competitive by both campaigns, it is not surprising that the campaigns tended to give these states much more attention than the other states. These battleground states saw more campaign offices, candidate appearances, campaign spending, and television advertising than did other states. Tables 4.2 and 4.3 provide a look at the number of campaign offices and candidate visits per state during the 2012 election (battleground states are bolded). It is pretty clear that some states receive a great deal of attention and some states receive virtually no attention from the campaigns. Because campaign resources are finite, campaigns have obvious reasons to maximize the impact of their resources. One interesting thing worth noting about battleground states versus non-battlegrounds is that "the abundance of campaign stimuli in campaign-rich battleground states sensitizes voters to events and accentuates their impact."[14] In short, voters who live in competitive states are more responsive to campaign events like the conventions and debates. This makes a great deal of sense because in battleground states there is an extensive campaign infrastructure, which includes resources (e.g., money) and mechanisms (e.g., campaign staff, media coverage, etc.) to capitalize directly on opportunities (or defend against adversities) created by campaign developments. In short, campaigns can amplify and reinforce the impact of relevant events, which helps voters to process campaign developments and form, update, or crystallize candidate preferences.[15]

Table 4.2 Number of Campaign Field Offices in 2012 Presidential Election by State

State	Obama Offices	Romney Offices
Alabama	1	0
Alaska	1	0
Arizona	1	0
Arkansas	1	0
California	14	0
Colorado	**62**	**13**
Connecticut	2	0
Delaware	1	0
District of Columbia	1	0
Florida	**104**	**48**

State	Obama Offices	Romney Offices
Georgia	4	0
Hawaii	1	0
Idaho	1	0
Illinois	4	0
Indiana	1	0
Iowa	**67**	**14**
Kansas	1	0
Kentucky	1	0
Louisiana	1	0
Maine	3	1
Maryland	1	0
Massachusetts	2	0
Michigan	28	24
Minnesota	12	0
Mississippi	1	0
Missouri	2	8
Montana	2	0
Nebraska	1	1
Nevada	**26**	**12**
New Hampshire	**22**	**9**
New Jersey	1	0
New Mexico	13	8
New York	5	0
North Carolina	**54**	**24**
North Dakota	1	0
Ohio	**131**	**40**
Oklahoma	1	0
Oregon	7	0
Pennsylvania	54	25
Rhode Island	1	0
South Carolina	3	0
South Dakota	1	0
Tennessee	1	0
Texas	4	0
Utah	1	4
Vermont	1	0
Virginia	**61**	**29**
Washington	10	0
West Virginia	1	0
Wisconsin	**69**	**24**
Wyoming	1	0
Total	790	284

Note: Battleground states are bolded. Data from http://www.fairvote.org/research-and-analysis/blog/tracking-presidential-campaign-field-operations/.

Table 4.3 Presidential Campaign Visits in 2012 by State

State	Obama and Biden Visits, June 2012–November 2012	Romney and Ryan Visits, June 2012–November 2012
Alabama	0	1
Alaska	0	0
Arizona	0	2
Arkansas	0	2
California	18	21
Colorado	**17**	**25**
Connecticut	3	0
Delaware	2	0
District of Columbia	20	6
Florida	**43**	**46**
Georgia	2	3
Hawaii	0	0
Idaho	0	1
Illinois	9	5
Indiana	0	1
Iowa	**29**	**26**
Kansas	0	0
Kentucky	1	2
Louisiana	5	7
Maine	0	0
Maryland	5	0
Massachusetts	6	12
Michigan	3	10
Minnesota	7	2
Mississippi	0	2
Missouri	1	3
Montana	0	2
Nebraska	0	0
Nevada	**15**	**15**
New Hampshire	**18**	**13**
New Jersey	3	5
New Mexico	0	3
New York	26	18
North Carolina	**7**	**11**
North Dakota	0	0
Ohio	**55**	**69**
Oklahoma	0	0
Oregon	2	3
Pennsylvania	8	16
Rhode Island	0	0
South Carolina	0	3
South Dakota	1	0
Tennessee	0	1

State	Obama and Biden Visits, June 2012–November 2012	Romney and Ryan Visits, June 2012–November 2012
Texas	6	12
Utah	1	5
Vermont	0	0
Virginia	**30**	**42**
Washington	4	2
West Virginia	0	0
Wisconsin	**17**	**14**
Wyoming	0	2
Total	364	413

Note: Battleground states are bolded. Data from *The Washington Post*, http://www.washingtonpost.com/wp-srv/special/politics/2012-presidential-campaign-visits/.

Election Outcomes: Who Wins and Why

Although presidential campaigns are complex events that take place over a fairly long period of time, political scientists have identified a number of factors that matter a great deal in determining the outcome. In order to understand presidential elections, it is important to have some sense of "the fundamentals," or the economic and political conditions that set the stage for presidential campaigns. If one has a good read on the fundamentals, it is usually possible to develop a good understanding of what might happen during any presidential election.

In general, political scientists typically start analyzing presidential elections by assessing incumbency and economic conditions, plus the salient events or attitudes that might impact how the public views the candidates. In U.S. elections at all levels, incumbents have tremendous advantages. They are better known than challengers, typically have more resources, and get a great deal of media attention while they are serving in office. When incumbent presidents run for reelection, they win about two-thirds of the time.[16] Thus, it is important to determine whether an incumbent president is involved in the election. We should point out that a number of issues can contribute to poor performance for an incumbent president. For example, if approval ratings are low or can be taken down by a poor economy, a losing war, or a well-known scandal, the incumbent party can lose.

In addition to incumbency, one of the most important factors to understand during presidential election years is the state of the economy. Political scientists and campaign professionals have long known that the state of the national economy plays a key role in shaping presidential elections. If you could pick only one variable to use to forecast presidential election outcomes, the state of the economy would be a great choice. A number of economic indicators correlate highly with presidential election outcomes, including change in disposable income and change in gross domestic product (GDP). When economic conditions are good, the incumbent party tends to be rewarded by voters. The electorate seems to be persuaded by the sentiment, as Ronald Reagan famously phrased it, "Are you better off than you were four years ago?" The reverse is also true: When economic conditions are poor, the incumbent party tends to be punished.[17] There is a very strong correlation between economic conditions and incumbent party vote share in U.S. presidential elections.

Although economic conditions are very important in presidential elections, a number of political factors can also impact presidential elections. Presidential approval is an important consideration. If an incumbent president has a high level of public approval before the election, the incumbent's chance of winning reelection is higher than if the incumbent suffers from a low level of public approval.[18] Another important political factor that can impact presidential elections is whether the country is involved in a war. If there is an ongoing war that the public perceives is going poorly, the incumbent president or party may be punished on Election Day. If there is an ongoing war that the public thinks is justified or going well, the incumbent may be rewarded on Election Day.

It turns out that presidential elections are highly predictable based on these fundamentals, leading some observers to conclude that campaigns may be irrelevant. If economic and political conditions matter so much during presidential elections, how could the campaigns possibly have any effects on voters or the election outcome? While it is certainly true that the fundamentals exert a significant pull on elections, it is important to keep in mind that campaigns often play a key role in shaping how voters perceive the fundamentals and in shaping how much weight voters put on each factor like the economy, incumbency, war, and presidential approval. Because voters tend to be ill informed about politics, campaigns can play an important role in educating voters about political and economic conditions. If a candidate is advantaged by economic conditions and his or her campaign consistently talks about the economy, it may become easier for voters to make this connection. Thus, campaigns can shape how voters connect the fundamentals to their votes.[19] There is good evidence that it can be very harmful when a campaign

66

fails to attach favorable economic conditions to their candidate in voters' minds. Many political scientists believe this happened during the 2000 election.[20] Although Gore was not the incumbent candidate, he was connected to the incumbent party as the vice president under Bill Clinton. During the years leading up to the election, the U.S. economy was doing quite well. Thus, Gore was advantaged by the underlying economic conditions. Interestingly, the Gore campaign seemed to downplay the economy on the campaign trail. Political scientists suspect that if the Gore campaign had done a better job connecting the economy to their candidate, he might have done better on Election Day.

Another important factor in determining the outcome is the level of financing available to the campaign. In recent presidential elections, the amount of money spent by the campaigns and allied groups has been remarkably high. The 2012 presidential election set a record: According to the Federal Election Commission, the total amount of money spent during the election was about $7 billion.[21] The Obama campaign spent about $1.12 billion and the Romney campaign about $1.02 billion. PACs spent about $1.2 billion and Super PACs spent about $950 million.

In some ways, the need for presidential candidates' campaigns to raise such vast sums of money is a relatively new phenomenon. Since the 1976 election cycle, a federal program of public financing has been in place to help minimize the disparities in access to campaign funds and level the playing field between presidential contenders. This is the only form of public financing available to federal candidates, and it is available for both the nomination and general election phase of the campaign. In the primary phase, candidates can become eligible for federal matching funds by raising more than $5,000 in each of at least 20 states (with only up to $250 per individual counting toward the threshold). Once eligible, the federal government will match up to $250 of an individual's total contributions. Funds to support this program do not come from tax receipts; instead, the program is financed through small ($3) voluntary, tax check-offs provided by taxpayers.

Sounds like a good deal, right? Nothing wrong with free money. But (you guessed it! no free lunch) there's a catch: There are strings attached to receiving these funds. Candidates must agree to limit personal spending to $50,000 and also to an aggregate national spending limit (in 2012, $45.6 million). Perhaps more importantly, the system imposes state-by-state spending limits based on state population. Above we discuss the overwhelming importance of early-voting states like Iowa and New Hampshire, but these are also small states in terms of population. So candidates who accepted public financing in the 2012 primaries would have been limited to spending $1.7 million in Iowa and $912,400 in New Hampshire. Although candidates would like the infusion of cash for their campaigns, they do not want to be bound by these restrictions. After working more or less as intended for two decades, the system began to collapse in the 1990s as candidates capable of raising large sums of campaign funds on their own began to opt out of the system. In 1996, publishing magnate and presidential candidate Steve Forbes rejected public financing; in subsequent cycles, most of the more viable contenders started opting out. In the general election, a lump sum is provided to each of the major-party nominees (in 2012, $91.2 million was available to each candidate), but their campaigns cannot raise or spend beyond that (there are no state-by-state limits). All major-party nominees had accepted general election funds since 1976, but in 2008, Barack Obama became the first candidate to reject public funding in the general election as well as in the primary. As a result, Obama's campaign was able to raise and spend $336 million in the general election, vastly outspending his opponent, Republican John McCain, who was limited to spending the $84.1 million he received from the program. Neither Obama nor Romney accepted public funding in the 2012 cycle.

When campaigns have similar amounts of resources, their efforts can offset each other. This does not mean, however, that campaigns and campaign resources are unimportant. Although campaigns may have equal amounts of money, they may adopt different strategies on how to use that money during the campaign. It is certainly possible that one candidate may use campaign dollars more strategically or effectively than his or her opponent. Of course, when there are disparities between campaigns in the amount of resources they have, campaign efforts can matter a great deal. During the 2008 election, for example, the Obama campaign had significantly more resources than the McCain campaign—Obama spent $730 million while McCain spent $333 million.[22] The Obama campaign set up a large number of campaign offices across the United States and bought a large number of advertising spots. One analysis found that "the Obama campaign gained a measurable electoral benefit in these states from its huge advantages in spending and field organization. That electoral benefit may well have tipped two states, Indiana and North Carolina, to Obama."[23] We should also note that campaigns can play an important role in shaping election outcomes when candidates are running behind where they are expected to be based on the fundamentals. In addition, campaigns can matter a great deal when fundamental conditions do not overwhelmingly favor one side.[24] Indeed, the messages that campaigns adopt and disseminate to the electorate can be decisive under certain conditions.

Campaign Events: Nominating Conventions and Debates

Many political scientists, including the authors of this book (both of whom study campaigns), have identified the effects of a number of campaign events on U.S. presidential elections. The two events that garner the most attention during presidential elections are the nominating conventions and candidate debates. In general, the conventions typically have larger effects on election outcomes than the debates. In large part, this has to do with the timing. The nominating conventions occur at the beginning of the general election campaign season (usually in the summer months) when voter preferences are not solidified. In addition, the conventions are the largest events of the campaigns and attract vast (though decreasing) amounts of media and public attention.

For over a century, conventions were typically raucous and unpredictable affairs that pitted candidates and camps of supporters against each other in vying for the presidential nominations. Often, there were no clear front-runners going into the nominating conventions, so political horse trading among party leaders in proverbial smoke-filled rooms was commonplace. At the Democratic convention held in Madison Square Garden in New York City in 1924, for example, delegates voted 103 times before former Ambassador to the United Kingdom John Davis secured the presidential nomination. Modern conventions are much less sensational. For starters, candidates have typically secured enough delegates during primaries and caucuses to enter the conventions as presumptive nominees, making the events far less newsworthy. In the television era, parties want to project the image of a unified party, largely for the benefit of viewing audiences, so they tend to be heavily scripted, upbeat, and positive. In a sense, they look much like giant pep rallies for the party and the nominees. The positive press coverage generally results in a boost in candidate support for the host party's nominees. Studies find convention bumps can vary in magnitude from just a few to more than 25 percentage points, averaging around 12 percentage points over the past few decades; moreover, the boosts in support tend to endure over the course of the campaign.[25] This is one reason why conventions remain important even though the presumptive nominees are typically known well before the start of contemporary conventions. Another reason conventions retain their significance is because the affairs elevate media coverage of the presidential campaign, energize party supporters, and focus the public's attention on the general election that follows. In recent cycles, about 10–15% of Americans make up their minds about which candidate to support on Election Day during the conventions, more so than during any other singular campaign event.[26]

Presidential debates, on the other hand, typically exert much smaller effects. The debates usually occur late in the campaign season when many voters have already made up their minds. Thus, there is limited potential for the debates to sway the electorate. Indeed, political scientist Thomas Holbrook found that across "16 presidential debates the average absolute change in candidate support was just less than 1 percentage point."[27] This doesn't mean that all debates are inconsequential, but it does suggest that, on average, presidential debates tend to have fairly limited effects on candidate support. Nevertheless, these effects do not always dissipate entirely and have the potential to shape voting preferences.

Overall, analyses of pre-election polls tend to show that preferences do not change dramatically over the course of a campaign (just a few percentage points up or down), but these shifts can be meaningful and persist to Election Day, helping to shape outcomes. Importantly, the timing of campaign events matters a great deal to voter preferences. Events that occur early on during presidential elections can have a stronger impact on voter preferences, but those effects are usually short-lived. Events that occur during the final 100 days of the campaign tend to exert smaller effects on voter preferences than early events, but the effects tend to persist and influence the outcome of the election.[28] In a close election, small changes in voter preferences could matter a great deal to the final outcome.

The role of campaign advertising also garners attention during elections. Campaigns now spend vast sums of money on television ads. But do television ads actually have an impact on voters? In general, political scientists have found that campaign ads can exert a persuasive effect on voters and can impact candidate vote share. When candidates spend more on television advertising than their opponents, they tend to perform better on Election Day.[29] In addition, exposure to campaign ads can influence individual vote choice.[30] The more campaign ads that one sees for a particular candidate, the more likely one is to vote for that candidate. Thus, it makes sense that campaigns would want to have an advantage when it comes to advertisements. We should note that the messages contained in campaign ads can be quite important. Some messages resonate with voters while others do not. If campaigns or allied groups can find a message that captures voter attention, campaign advertisements can be quite influential. Two ads created against Democrat John Kerry in the 2004 presidential election stand out as recent examples. An ad created and broadcasted by the group Swift Boat Veterans for Truth attempted to discredit Kerry's heroism as a swiftboat commander in the Vietnam War. Although the ad was later discredited, the term "swiftboating" emerged as a pejorative neologism to describe unfair but effective political attacks. During the same cycle, the Bush campaign ran an ad featuring footage of Kerry windsurfing while on vacation in Nantucket; as the sail flailed back and forth in the gust, the ad simultaneously provided a visual image to reinforce that Kerry was a flip-flopper (Kerry famously said that he "voted for the Iraq War before voting against it") and that his affluence disconnected him from average Americans (like squash, sailing, and polo, windsurfing is widely viewed as a sport for the rich).

Ways to Improve Presidential Elections

As we did in the previous chapters, we would like to end by providing some ideas on how presidential elections in the United States could be improved.

- As we mentioned in Chapter 2, many citizens do not participate in presidential elections. This is especially true when it comes to primaries and caucuses. Citizens need to start taking advantage of the opportunities for political input that already exist in our system. The ideas discussed in Chapter 2 may provide some guidance on how to increase voter engagement during presidential elections.
- If citizens are unhappy with how presidential elections are funded, they could pressure legislators to adopt new campaign finance programs. A number of interesting proposals are currently getting some attention in the United States. Lawrence Lessig, a law professor, has suggested something that he calls "democracy vouchers." He notes that "almost every voter pays at least $50 in some form of federal taxes. So imagine a system that gave a rebate of that first $50 in the form of a 'democracy voucher.' That voucher could then be given to any candidate for Congress who agreed to one simple condition: the only money that candidate would accept to finance his or her campaign would be either 'democracy vouchers' or contributions from citizens capped at $100. No PAC money. No $2,500 checks. Small contributions only. And if the voter didn't use the voucher? The money would pass to his or her party, or, if an independent, back to this public funding system."[31] This idea could certainly be applied to presidential elections. Although campaign finance is not a salient political issue, there are interesting ideas out there that could address some of the key issues that people have.

- Citizens often complain about being uninformed about presidential politics or about the difficulty in finding good information. Scholars Bruce Ackerman and James Fishkin have proposed a holiday called "Deliberation Day." The logic behind this new holiday is simple: On Deliberation Day people throughout the United States would meet in public spaces (one week before presidential elections) and engage in debates about political issues and the candidates featured in the upcoming presidential election. The holiday would feature a small reward of $150 for each deliberator, on the condition that deliberators vote in the presidential election.[32]

- Many analysts believe the system of presidential public funding described above is defunct. To begin with, Americans appear to be increasingly less supportive of the program. According to the Federal Election Commission, fewer than 7% of American taxpayers contributed to the fund in 2010, down from about 30% in the 1980s. With most of the competitive presidential contenders opting out in recent cycles, many question whether the program's usefulness is outlived. In principle, however, the spirit of the program (leveling the playing field, allowing candidates to focus on voters rather than fundraising) remains intact. If we believe the presidential public funding system is worth rescuing, several reform options have been proposed. The national spending limits in both the primary and general elections could be raised, for instance, or adjustments could be made to statewide spending limits in the primary phase to take into account the practical importance of early-voting states like Iowa or New Hampshire. Some have also proposed a more generous matching formula in the primary (a $4-to-$1 match, for example, rather than the $1-to-$1 formula currently in place or matching more of each individual contribution) to provide access to more funding, making the system more attractive to presidential candidates. Such reforms could revive the system and help it to achieve its original goals.

- Studies have documented that turnout is lower in caucuses than primaries and that caucuses attract ideologically extreme participants. Given such concerns, it may be reasonable to abandon caucuses in favor of primaries. Though primaries are not perfect, they are likely to elevate participation in primary elections and to attract electorates that are more representative of the broader electorate.

- If citizens are unhappy with the Electoral College, they could use features within our system to make changes. State legislatures are charged with determining how their state's electoral votes will be allocated. It is certainly possible that states could alter their procedures if citizens are displeased with them. There is currently something called the National Popular Vote Interstate Compact, which is an agreement among ten states and Washington, D.C., to allocate their electors to the winner of the national popular vote (rather than to the winner of the popular vote of their particular state, which is what the current system does). Although this may not be the exact system that citizens ultimately decide on, it does illustrate that our system provides mechanisms for citizens to alter things they dislike.

Notes

1. Panagopoulos, Costas. 2010. "Are Caucuses Bad for Democracy?" *Political Science Quarterly* 125: 425–442.
2. Wattier, Mark. 2004. "Presidential Primaries and Frontloading: An Empirical Polemic." Paper presented at the "State of the Party: 2004 & Beyond."
3. Wattier, Mark. 2004. "Presidential Primaries and Frontloading: An Empirical Polemic." Paper presented at the "State of the Party: 2004 & Beyond."
4. Panagopoulos, Costas. 2008. "Presidential Nominating Conventions: Past, Present, and Future." *The Forum* 5: 1–12.
5. http://www.bloombergview.com/articles/2014-07-22/chuck-schumer-gets-primaries-all-wrong.
6. Cohen, Marty, David Karol, Hans Noel, and John Zaller. 2008. *The Party Decides: Presidential Nominations Before and After Reform.* Chicago, IL: University of Chicago Press.
7. http://www.gallup.com/poll/150245/americans-swap-electoral-college-popular-vote.aspx.
8. Panagopoulos, Costas. 2004. "The Polls—Trends: Electoral Reform." *Public Opinion Quarterly* 68 (4): 623–641.
9. http://www.fairvote.org/reforms/national-popular-vote/the-electoral-college/electoral-college-faqs/.
10. http://avalon.law.yale.edu/18th_century/fed68.asp.
11. http://thomas.loc.gov/home/histdox/fed_68.html.
12. Shaw, Daron. 2006. *The Race to 270: The Electoral College and the Campaign Strategies of 2000 and 2004.* Chicago, IL: University of Chicago Press.
13. http://www.washingtonpost.com/blogs/the-fix/post/the-9-swing-states-of-2012/2012/04/16/gIQABuXaLT_blog.html.
14. Panagopoulos, Costas. 2012. "Campaign Context and Preference Dynamics in U.S. Presidential Elections." *Journal of Elections, Public Opinion and Parties* 22: 123–137.
15. Panagopoulos, Costas. 2012. "Campaign Context and Preference Dynamics in U.S. Presidential Elections." *Journal of Elections, Public Opinion and Parties* 22: 123–137.

16. Sides, John, and Lynn Vavreck. 2012. *The Gamble: Choice and Chance in the 2012 Presidential Election.* Princeton, NJ: Princeton University Press.
17. Fiorina, Morris. 1981. *Retrospective Voting in American National Elections.* New Haven, CT: Yale.
18. Holbrook, Thomas. 2004. "Good News for Bush? Economic News, Personal Finances, and the 2004 Presidential Election." *PS: Political Science and Politic* October: 759–761.
19. McClurg, Scott, and Thomas Holbrook. 2009. "Living in a Battleground: Presidential Campaigns and Fundamental Predictors of Vote Choice." *Political Research Quarterly* 62: 495–506.
20. Fiorina, Morris, Samuel Abrams, and Jeremy Pope. 2003. "The 2000 US Presidential Election: Can Retrospective Voting Be Saved?" *British Journal of Political Science* 48: 723–741.
21. http://www.fec.gov/portal/presidential.shtml.
22. https://www.opensecrets.org/pres08/.
23. http://www.centerforpolitics.org/crystalball/articles/do-presidential-campaigns-matter-evidence-from-the-2008-election/.
24. Holbrook, Thomas. 1996. *Do Campaigns Matter?* Thousand Oaks, CA: Sage.
25. Panagopoulos, Costas, ed. 2007. *Rewiring Politics: Presidential Nominating Conventions in the Media Age.* Baton Rouge, LA: Louisiana State University Press; Stimson, James. 2004. *Tides of Consent: How Public Opinion Shapes American Politics.* New York, NY: Cambridge University Press; Panagopoulos, Costas. 2008. "Presidential Nominating Conventions: Past, Present, and Future." *The Forum* 5: 1–12.
26. Panagopoulos, Costas, ed. 2007. *Rewiring Politics: Presidential Nominating Conventions in the Media Age.* Baton Rouge, LA: Louisiana State University Press; Panagopoulos, Costas. 2008. "Presidential Nominating Conventions: Past, Present, and Future." *The Forum* 5: 1–12.
27. http://www.huffingtonpost.com/thomas-m-holbrook/debate-expectations_b_1930043.html.
28. Wlezien, Christopher, and Robert Erikson 2002. "The Timeline of Presidential Election Campaigns." *Journal of Politics* 64: 969–993.
29. Shaw, Daron. 1999. "The Effect of TV Ads and Candidate Appearances on Statewide Presidential Votes, 1988–96." *American Political Science Review* 93: 345–361.
30. Franz, Michael, and Travis Ridout. 2007. "Does Political Advertising Persuade?" *Political Behavior* 29: 465–491.
31. http://www.nytimes.com/2011/11/17/opinion/in-campaign-financing-more-money-can-beat-big-money.html?_r=0.
32. Ackerman, Bruce, and James Fishkin. 2004. *Deliberation Day.* New Haven, CT: Yale University Press.

5

CONGRESSIONAL ELECTIONS

At the end of November 2012, a poll conducted by CBS News and *The New York Times* found that only 15% of Americans approved of the job Congress was doing, while 75% disapproved. Most other prominent national polls showed similar splits. A little more than a week later, during the national election, 90% of the members of the U.S. House of Representatives seeking reelection—and 91% of the Senate incumbents—were reelected in districts and states across the country.

These results are not unusual; incumbents have routinely been returned to Congress at rates above 90% over the past few decades. Since 1964, the reelection rate for U.S. House members has never dipped below 85%, with the average being 93%. In many of the House elections over this period, over 95% of U.S. House incumbents have been reelected. Even in "bad years" for incumbents, they win at high rates. During the 2010 mid-term elections, which followed the 2009 government shutdown, voters reelected 85% of House incumbents. Reelection rates for Senate incumbents have also been high, although they are a bit more variable, ranging from 55% to 96%, with the average being 82% from 1964 to 2012. The graphs shown in Figures 5.1 and 5.2 highlight these trends.

Over the past decade, no reputable national poll has registered majority approval of Congress. In most polls conducted over this period, strong majorities *disapprove* of Congress's performance. Congressional approval even reached a historic low (9%) in November 2013.[1] Americans have a range of reasons for their disapproval of the U.S. Congress. A Gallup poll conducted in June 2013 sheds a great deal of light on the key objections that people have, illustrated in Table 5.1. It is clear that the lack of productivity is an important part of why people say they are so dissatisfied. We return to the issue of gridlock in Congress in a section that follows. To be clear, public opinion polls consistently show that people view their own congressional representatives

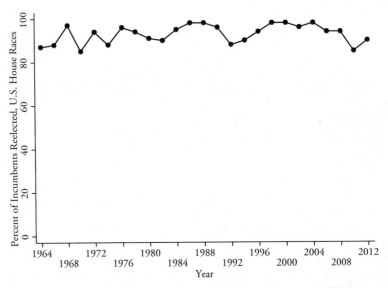

Figure 5.1 Reelection Rates for Incumbents in U.S. House Elections, 1964–2012. Data from https://www.opensecrets.org.

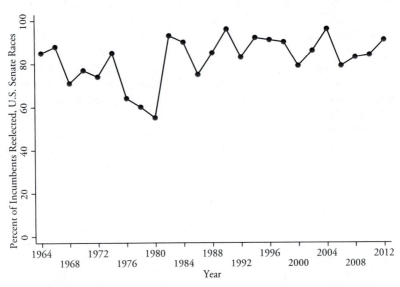

Figure 5.2 Reelection Rates for Incumbents in U.S. Senate Elections, 1964–2012. Data from https://www.opensecrets.org.

far more favorably than the institution as a whole.[2] Indeed, according to a 2013 Gallup poll, 46% of people approved of the job performance of the representative from their district. And, among those who could provide that person's name, 62% approved.[3] Despite the fact that Americans tend to view their own representatives much more favorably than Congress as a whole, it is still difficult to reconcile the alarmingly low Congress approval ratings with the sky-high reelection rates. How is it possible that so few Americans approve of Congress's performance but yet so few incumbents lose their reelection bids?

Table 5.1 Top Reasons Why Americans Disapprove of Congress

Reason	Percent of People Who Listed This Reason
Party gridlock/Bickering/Not compromising	28%
Not getting anything done/ Not making decisions	21%
Caring too much about politics, not about country	11%
Budget deficit/Spending	6%
Not supporting the president	5%
Not doing a good job/Don't like what they are doing/Wrong policies	4%
Exhibiting a lack integrity/Dishonesty	4%

Note: Data from Gallup June 1–4, 2013, poll.

Explaining the Incumbency Advantage

Scholars have identified many reasons why incumbents are so favored—a tendency termed "incumbency advantage" by political scientists. To be clear, incumbents are not just advantaged in congressional elections. At all levels of government, incumbent candidates win at extremely high rates.[4] Some of the reasons for the congressional incumbency advantage are structural. Redistricting processes held every 10 years after the U.S. census often carve out districts that are favorable to incumbents, at least in elections for the U.S. House of Representatives (there is not redistricting in U.S. Senate elections); committee assignments allow members of Congress to develop expertise and relationships that help to bring benefits back to their districts; and elected officials benefit from greater name recognition because they often receive media attention for the work they do while in office. Incumbents also leverage their power and resources to build relationships and to assist constituents with various needs, enabling them to cultivate what scholars have termed a "personal vote" that favors them in elections. Indeed, one recent commentary on congressional elections pointed out that "voters elect solely their own representatives, and their ballots aren't necessarily a referendum on the entire legislative body."[5] It is much easier to dislike an institution than it is an individual person. If voters are familiar with their district's representative—and research has shown that voters are much more familiar with congressional incumbents than challengers due to the resources and media attention they garner— they are much more likely to support them on Election Day.[6]

An important part of the story about why incumbents are advantaged in elections also centers on money. Incumbents typically raise and spend significantly more money than their challengers. Figures 5.3 and 5.4 show the average amounts of money spent by the two kinds of candidates in congressional elections over time. It is clear that incumbents consistently outspend challengers and that the spending gap has increased over time. In 2012, the average spending by House incumbents was $1.7 million compared to the $587,000 by House challengers. In other words, incumbents outspent their challengers by a ratio of about 3 to 1. Senate incumbents in 2012 spent an average of $10.7 million while challengers spent an average of only $7.2 million. Incumbents have also generally attracted large percentages of PAC money in recent years.[7] PACs or political action committees are simply groups that raise and spend money to help elect candidates they prefer (or defeat candidates they do not favor). In recent election cycles, upwards of 80% of PAC money went to incumbents. Some incumbents have even received a majority of their campaign funding from PACs.[8] According to a 2010 report on PAC money in congressional elections, "more than one in five House incumbents has collected 60 percent or more of their war chest from PACs."[9] Money is an important resource during campaigns, and incumbents typically have an easier time collecting it because they are a safer investment. As one journalist pointed out in the context of the 2010 congressional elections, "Incumbency may be a bad word among this year's angry voters, but it translates into power in Washington. And power gets money, regardless of party."[10] Indeed, campaign donors are strategic—they want to maximize their chances of getting access and influence—so they tend to give to candidates whom they believe will be a sound investment.

We should point out that one of the most consistent findings from political science research on the effects of campaign spending is that although incumbents typically far outspend their challengers, incumbent spending is far less influential than challenger spending. The money spent by challengers has a much more pronounced effect on vote share in congressional elections, presumably because challengers are much less known than incumbents and their campaign spending provides new information to the electorate. Of course, the difficulty for challengers is to be able to raise and spend large sums of money.[11] This is something that many challengers are unable to do.

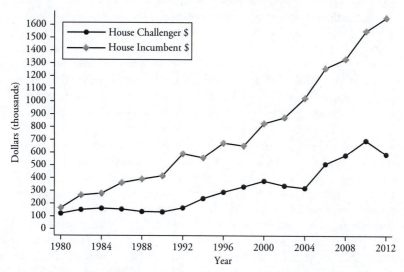

Figure 5.3 Campaign Spending in U.S. House Elections, 1980–2012. Data from https://www.opensecrets.org.

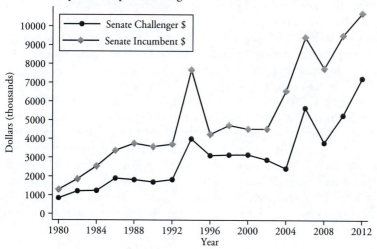

Figure 5.4 Campaign Spending in U.S. Senate Elections, 1980–2012. Data from https://www.opensecrets.org.

It is often hard to know if incumbents win by such wide margins (in U.S. House elections, incumbents have averaged at least 60% of the two-party vote since 1950) because voters really like them or simply because the system provides so many advantages to them that it is nearly impossible for challengers to overcome these barriers. It is interesting to note that voters tend to be poorly informed about congressional candidates and their policy positions. Political scientist Joshua Darr has found that just 14.5% of voters can recall the name of their incumbent and just 4.9% can recall challengers.[12] When thinking about incumbent reelection rates, it is interesting to consider things from the standpoint of a candidate who is considering challenging a congressional incumbent. At least on some level, incumbency is a powerful advantage that prospective challengers are unwilling to go up against. Incumbents routinely face only token opposition, if any at all. Indeed, in the 2014 congressional primaries, "most of the House candidates, about 60 percent so far, didn't have a soul running against them. Only a few faced a challenger who posed a real threat."[13] Studies show that the "quality" of challengers facing incumbents in elections is a key determinant of incumbent performance; contests that involve incumbents facing experienced or otherwise "high-quality" challengers (who have held previous elective office) are typically more competitive than those in which only inexperienced (or "low-quality") challengers emerge to raise a challenge. The problem is that not many "high-quality" challengers are willing to face off against incumbents. Over the past few decades, fewer and fewer high-quality challengers have been tossing their hats into the ring. It is not uncommon for only about one in five incumbents seeking reelection to be up against a high-quality challenger during the general election. Is it any wonder, then, that so many of these incumbents win?

One journalist recently summarized congressional elections in the following way: "Americans might be mad as hell at Congress—but they're going to keep taking it."[14] Another analysis pointed out that measures of congressional approval are at "historic lows" and even approval levels of individual representatives are "below 50 percent. But that doesn't mean most of Congress is going to be turned out; in fact, a vast majority of members of Congress are going to get reelected."[15] Indeed, given the trends shown in Figures 5.1 and 5.2, there is no sign that incumbents are going to starting losing at high rates.

Polarization, Gridlock, and Dissatisfaction with Congress

It is interesting to consider what ordinary Americans think could be done to make Congress better. Despite the high incumbent reelection rates, Table 5.1 illustrated that citizens have a range of complaints about Congress. In a 2014 poll, Gallup asked a representative sample of Americans a simple question: "What is the most important thing that you would recommend be done to fix Congress?" Survey respondents were able to provide any idea that they wanted, since the question was open-ended. The top results from the poll are shown in Table 5.2. Interestingly, a number of ideas received a fair amount of support from the American public. For example, 22% of people said that the most important fix would be to fire or replace all members, 14% of people said that more bipartisan cooperation is needed, 11% of people said that term limits or shorter terms are needed, and 9% of people said that we need to make members accountable to the people rather than their own agendas. It is quite thought provoking to learn about the kinds of things that Americans think would make Congress better and to consider those "fixes" alongside congressional election results. Interestingly, many of the proposed solutions stand in contrast to outcomes we see in congressional elections. If firing or replacing all members would help fix Congress, why are incumbents reelected at such high rates every year? If more bipartisan cooperation is needed, why do voters keep electing politicians who are becoming more ideologically distant over time? If members of Congress are accountable to their own agendas and not the people, why do Americans keep returning the same politicians to office over and over again? If congressional gridlock is such a concern to so many people, why reelect people who do not contribute policy ideas or bills to Congress for consideration? Although Americans regularly complain about Congress's performance, it is important to note that what happens in congressional elections has a lot to do with the outcomes and performance that we get out of Congress. In the sections that follow, we discuss some of the pressing concerns that people have about the modern U.S. Congress and how citizens might be able to change some of things they dislike.

One topic that has captured a great deal of attention recently is that of party polarization in Congress. Scholars have convincingly demonstrated that the major parties have become increasingly ideologically polarized over the last several decades.[16] In other words, the Democratic and Republican

Table 5.2 Ideas on How to Fix Congress

What Should Be Done	Percent of People Who Listed This Reason
Fire/Replace all members/ Get all new people	22%
More bipartisan cooperation/ Work together/Get along better	14%
Set term limits/Shorten terms	11%
Make members accountable to the people, not their own agendas	9%
Regulate campaign finances/Limit special interest contributions	3%
Follow the Constitution/Live by the rules	3%
Reduce the influence of parties/ Get a third party/More independents	3%
Change the benefit/pay structure	2%

Note: Data from Gallup July 7–1 0, 2014, poll.

parties are ideologically distinct (the Democratic Party has become more liberal over time and the Republican Party has become more conservative over time), so the distance between the parties has been growing. One commentary on party polarization pointed out that "it is now safe to say that polarization in Congress has reached an all-time high, exceeding even levels seen during the late nineteenth century."[17] Public opinion studies have consistently shown that the American public views polarization, the lack of bipartisan cooperation in Congress, and legislative gridlock negatively. It is interesting to note that party polarization and gridlock are related in an important way. Political scientist Sarah Binder notes that "as legislative 'moderation' declines, Congress and the president frequently deadlock over the salient issues of the day ... When centrist legislators populate a Congress backed by relatively centrist parties, legislative agreement is frequently in reach on the big issues of the day. As more lawmakers move away from the political center and the parties diverge ideologically, Congress deadlocks more often."[18]

Binder goes on to provide two ideas about why polarization and gridlock are positively related. First, the U.S. political system generally requires broad coalitions of legislators to create large policy changes. It's simply easier to assemble a broad coalition when there is a large number of legislators who are moderate and can bridge ideological divides. Second, when elites and activists are politically polarized (as they currently are), members of Congress often try to differentiate their positions and ideologies and they have a lesser incentive to compromise.

When coupled with divided government (when one party controls the presidency while the other controls Congress) and divided houses of Congress (when the Senate and House of Representative are controlled by different parties), polarization in Congress makes it difficult for legislators to create policy.

Although there is widespread agreement among researchers that the major parties have polarized over time, there are a number of different ideas about what has driven party polarization. One interesting account focuses on the role of political activists. Activists are "the people most energized by the movement's agenda. Activists are not just voters who are sympathetic to the movement, nor are they necessarily the leaders of the movement. They are the ones willing to take some action for the cause."[19] As political scientist Hans Noel recently pointed out, "Members of Congress are not polarized because voters are now better sorted. And voters are not polarized simply because legislators now are. The missing piece is ideological activists, who now dominate the political parties—in short, policy demanders. These politically engaged activists are the base that legislators are increasingly playing to, because they are the ones who provide campaign resources and who threaten primary challenges. Their polarization also filters to voters, through elected officials but also through the media and informal networks."[20] It is important to note that political activists appear to have become more polarized on a range of issues over time.[21] Indeed, one study of political activists found that increases in activist polarization on a range of political issues have coincided with the growth of party differences on those issues in Congress.[22]

Political scientists are working to learn more about the activists who increasingly influence politics. One recent movement—the Tea Party—provides some sense of how activists can have important effects on congressional elections and policymaking. The Tea Party is a conservative political movement that first emerged in 2009 and attempted to influence the 2010 congressional elections. While people who affiliate with the Tea Party tend to back a range of conservative issue positions, the movement is focused on fiscal restraint, advocating lower taxes, less government spending, and addressing the national debt. During the 2010 elections, there were a number of Tea Party–affiliated groups across the United States, which attracted a great deal of support from political activists (and ordinary voters in some cases) in some U.S. congressional districts. In a 2012 study on the Tea Party, researchers found that the number of Tea Party activists in congressional districts had important effects on the 2010 congressional elections as well as on the voting patterns of individual members of Congress following the elections. For example, those Republican candidates who ran in districts that had high numbers of Tea Party activists did better in the 2010 general election than other Republican candidates.[23] Activists within movements like the Tea Party tend to be enthusiastic supporters of their preferred candidates—they campaign hard for those they want elected and they campaign hard against candidates they dislike. Thus, it makes sense that Republicans who had the support of Tea Party activists outperformed those who did not have support. The same study (by Bailey, Mummolo, and Noel) found that on votes that were of concern to the Tea Party, those members of Congress who came from districts with high numbers of Tea Party activists voted on issues in ways that were consistent with what the movement wanted (e.g., debt, budget issues, etc.). The authors nicely summarize the role of the Tea Party in the 2010 elections as a movement of activists, or "not a simple reflection of the will of the people. Its impact appears to have required mobilization among activists. Members of Congress are not responding to changes in the preferences of constituents so much as they are responding to an organized interest, and one that put electoral and legislative politics at the top of its agenda."[24]

Regardless of whether one agrees or disagrees with the Tea Party movement, this example showcases just how important political activists can be to congressional elections and to the policies that emerge from Congress after elections. Most of us have probably heard the phrase "the squeaky wheel gets the grease." This seems to be what happened during the 2010 congressional elections. The Tea Party movement made itself noticeable to Republican candidates and many were responsive to the preferences of Tea Party activists following the elections. Due to its involvement in recent House and Senate elections, many political scientists agree that the Tea Party has moved the Republican Party further to the political right, which fits with the goals of activists associated with the movement.[25] In Chapter 2, we presented some basic information on levels of political participation in the United States, and in the introductory chapter we noted that when public opinion was strong and clear, citizens have influence—that intensity is the currency of American politics. The implication is that ordinary citizens need to be active participants in the political process—when they are not, candidates and policies are likely to be responsive to those who are the most politically active. Importantly, the preferences of political activists may differ from average citizens (Tea Party activists were more ideologically conservative than average citizens, as were their policy preferences).[26] If it is the case that activists hold different preferences than average Americans, then elected officials and the public policies they pursue may not represent typical citizens. The Tea Party example illustrates just how important intensity is in American political life. When groups and individuals make themselves politically relevant, and when they express their preferences by participating in politics intensely, politicians are likely to pay attention to them. Thus, it is particularly important that ordinary citizens participate in congressional primaries and general elections. In short, we need broad participation in congressional politics by the American public. As the Task Force on Inequality and American Democracy for the American Political Science Association has noted, "Not only are many citizens politically inactive, but the processes by which people come to take part imply that, taken together, activists are not representative of the American public and, thus, that public officials are disproportionately likely to hear from people with certain politically relevant characteristics."[27] We should point out that while the participation habits of ideological activists play an important role in American politics, biases in participation will tend to coincide with biases in political outcomes. Indeed, in many American cities, we see disparities in the participation rates of citizens with different backgrounds (e.g., race, income, profession, etc.). Oftentimes, the politicians who are elected and the policies they pursue are skewed in favor of those who participated in the political process.[28]

Another concern that has captured the attention of journalists, ordinary citizens, and scholars is *redistricting*. This is simply the process of carving states up into congressional districts, typically after the national census required by the Constitution every ten years for the purpose of reapportionment (assigning congressional seats to states based on their relative populations). One of the most concerning things about redistricting is the potential for gerrymandering, which refers to the process of drawing congressional district boundaries so that one political party (or group) is electorally advantaged over another. To be clear, gerrymandering is not a new phenomenon. It actually dates back to the 1800s in the United States. It is common these days to blame gerrymandering for many of the problems associated with congressional politics, especially political polarization. The basic reason for connecting gerrymandering and polarization is straightforward. As *The Washington Post* phrases it,

> First, by using the latest sophisticated software, state legislatures can carve out districts that guarantee electoral victory for one party or the other, often in the service of protecting incum-

bents. Generally, the gerrymanderers accomplish this by packing Republican voters into Republican districts and Democratic voters into Democratic districts. Second, because such gerrymandering makes the districts less competitive, candidates are freed to pander to their bases while ignoring moderate and independent voters. Moreover, politicians who do not pander face primary challenges from ideologically purer candidates. The result often is that only conservative Republicans can win in districts designed to elect Republicans, just as liberal Democrats usually dominate Democratic districts. Because redistricting no longer produces moderate, bipartisan or heterogeneous districts, moderates have trouble winning election to the House.[29]

This commonly held idea seems to make sense on the face of it. Interestingly, political scientists have shown that gerrymandering has actually had fairly limited effects on polarization. There are a number of observations that support this claim. Take polarization in the U.S. Senate as an example. The Senate is not subject to redistricting—all candidates are elected on a statewide basis—and yet parties in the Senate have become increasingly polarized over time, just as the parties in the U.S. House have. If redistricting doesn't occur in the Senate but the chamber has still become more polarized over the past several decades, how can gerrymandering be to blame? There is also evidence from political science studies that polarization largely occurs due to differences in how Democrats and Republicans representing similar districts behave.[30] Over time, more and more moderate districts have come to be represented by liberal Democrats and conservative Republicans. It's also the case that there are more liberal and conservative districts and fewer moderate ones now than in the past.

Part of the reason why we may see changes in the kinds of representatives being elected to Congress (more ideologically extreme members) is something that political scientists have called "leapfrog representation." This refers to the idea that when a member of Congress is replaced by a new member of the opposite party (usually because voters perceive the original member of Congress as being too extreme), we generally see one extreme representative replaced by another extreme representative.[31] This phenomenon has happened in recent election cycles, resulting in less moderation in Congress than average voters may desire. One thing that may be driving "leapfrogging" is the responsiveness of congressional candidates to activists. As we noted above, politicians tend to pay the greatest attention to those who are the most visible—the activists. Since political activists tend to be more polarized than those who do not participate in politics, this polarization might be reflected in the candidates who are selected in congressional elections.

It is conceivable that political polarization at the national level may discourage state-level candidates from running for higher office. A recent study by political scientist Danielle Thomsen found that polarization is at least partially shaped by which state legislators run for Congress.[32] Thomsen's research indicates that moderates who are serving in state legislatures are less likely to run when they see high levels of congressional polarization. In part, their fears stem from concerns about winning their primary (where they may have to appear more ideologically extreme than they actually are) or the general election. Ideological polarization may also lead moderates to believe that it will be hard to accomplish their legislative goals if they are elected to serve in Congress. It is, of course, quite costly to run for federal office, so it makes sense that these concerns might decrease the probability of ideological moderates running for Congress. This process creates a cycle where moderates are discouraged from running (due to observed levels of polarization) and because fewer moderates run (and are elected), levels of congressional polarization remain high or increase over time. Thomsen argues, "If we want to change the current course of congressional policymaking and end the gridlock in Washington, a good first step is for ideological moderates to launch political candidacies."[33]

Before we proceed to a discussion of potential solutions to the problems that people see with congressional politics, we should point out that although gerrymandering is often associated with obtaining a partisan advantage, there is some evidence that gerrymandering is done to protect incumbents. Indeed, political parties may want to bargain with each other in order to maintain the status quo. In short, the parties may cooperate to protect current incumbents and preserve existing constituencies. There are a number of potential effects of incumbent-protecting gerrymandering. For instance, the parties may be able to weed out new candidates who might challenge their incumbents. In addition, this kind of gerrymandering might make it difficult for newly emerging constituencies to compete in electoral politics. Although people tend to like it when electoral politics is competitive (and citizens participate at higher rates), it is not too difficult to understand why political parties might not want more electoral competition or unpredictability. As a final note, gerrymandering can also be done on the basis of racial considerations. In short, districts can be drawn or redrawn in an attempt to advantage or disadvantage particular racial groups. In some cases, redrawing district boundaries on the basis of race may be used for partisan purposes, but it is important to note that in some cases states are permitted (or required) to create majority-minority congressional districts (districts in which a minority group makes up the majority of the district). This is designed to ensure the representation of minority groups and increase the number of minority members of Congress. The idea of majority-minority districts comes from the Voting Rights Act and is one way of making sure that minority groups are able to secure representation in Congress.[34]

Midterm Losses in Congressional Elections

We conclude our discussion of congressional elections by returning to the midterms. Recall that all of the U.S. House seats and one-third of U.S. Senate seats (senators serve six-year terms) are up for election every two years. Accordingly, some of these occur in tandem with the presidential election, but congressional elections are also held between presidential election years (at the midterm of the presidential cycle). An empirical regularity that characterizes midterm elections, besides lower rates of participation discussed above, is that the party of the incumbent president tends to perform poorly during these cycles. This holds for both Democratic and Republican presidents. Over the postwar period, the party of the incumbent president has lost on average 27 seats in the House of Representatives and four seats in the Senate. In fact, the president's party has picked up seats in both chambers only once (in 2002, just after 9/11) over this period.

Political scientists have offered a range of explanations for the so-called "puzzle of midterm loss." James Campbell's theory of "surge-and-decline" goes something like this: The winning presidential party's congressional support surges in response to "short-term partisan forces" (for example, increased participation by the president's party members) in the "high-stimulus" presidential year; these waxing forces (or presidential "coattails") then wane in the following midterm election when the president is not on the ballot and the outcome returns to the "normal" (largely party-line) vote. "Referendum" theory, on the other hand, argues that the midterm slump results from voters' reactions to the erosion in presidential popularity that generally follows the honeymoon phase of a presidential term. A third line of reasoning claims that voters use midterms to pursue policy or ideological balancing by boosting support for the out party, a view supported by empirical evidence put forth by political scientists Joseph Bafumi, Robert Erikson, and

Christopher Wlezien.[35] Bafumi, Erikson, and Wlezien summarize midterm losses by noting, "We end up with two separate but compatible explanations for midterm loss. In presidential years, the winning presidential party is advantaged in the congressional elections, due to the surge/coattails phenomenon. This advantage is withdrawn in midterm election years. ... [A]t midterm the presidential party is disadvantaged, as the electorate shifts its preferences to the out party. Together these two components generate the regularity of midterm loss." At present, no clear, scholarly consensus has emerged to explain the midterm loss phenomenon, so the debate endures.

Ways to Improve Congressional Elections

As we did in the previous chapters, we would like to end by providing some ideas on how congressional elections in the United States could be improved.

- Citizens could take advantage of the tools at their disposal to make sure that their preferences are being represented. Political science research has indicated that very few people have contacted their congressional representatives to express their opinions, a fairly small slice of the population votes in congressional elections (especially primaries), and few people attend meetings with members of Congress. Increasing political engagement has the potential to reduce the influence of interest groups or activists (who tend to be more ideologically extreme than the average voter).
- Although greater access to data on the American population now permits more precise gerrymandering mischief, it is also important to note that it creates greater opportunities for public input and scrutiny. Redistricting is often seen as a technical process, unfolding behind the scenes with little public awareness or involvement. If people believe that more public input and scrutiny of redistricting plans would help increase confidence in the electoral process, they could pressure states to open up the redistricting process. In the state of Montana, the government holds hearings around the state to get the public's input on criteria that will be used to formulate new districts.[36] This could certainly be done in other places.
- There is great variation across states in the requirements for congressional candidates to get on the ballot. In places where the ballot access requirements are burdensome (e.g., large number of signatures required, large filing fee, etc.), it can be a barrier for minor-party

candidates. If citizens are interested in seeing additional parties contesting elections, citizens may want to investigate the ballot access requirement in their state. These requirements can be changed if citizens do not like how they are limiting electoral competition.

- There has been much concern about having state legislatures do redistricting. There are a variety of other mechanisms for redistricting, including nonpartisan commissions, independent (but partisan) commissions, or panels composed of retired judges. Interestingly, there is little evidence that using nonpartisan commissions (rather than the state legislature) increases public confidence in the redistricting process.[37] Perhaps it will be important to look for alternative ways to increase confidence, such as allowing for citizen input. The state of California has moved in this direction and now has a "Citizens Redistricting Commission," which features 14 members who "must draw the district lines in conformity with strict, nonpartisan rules designed to create districts of relatively equal population that will provide fair representation for all Californians. The Commission must hold public hearings and accept public comment."[38] While there is little evidence that redistricting has caused polarization, this type of reform could help boost public confidence in the electoral process.

- Many people have expressed concern about the declining number of moderates in Congress over time. Members of Congress are, of course, selected through elections, so the public plays a role in deciding who serves. Increasing the number of moderates is not a simple task, although there is evidence that it is possible to increase the likelihood that ideological extremists are voted out of office. Political scientist Seth Masket has noted that "ideologically extreme elected officials are more vulnerable to defeat where there is better journalistic coverage. They have greater incentive to behave as moderates if they know that voters are watching. So if you want more centrist elected officials, there's your reform: have journalists provide better coverage of politics."[39] There are a number of ways to increase monitoring. For instance, voters could contact local media outlets and urge them to devote more coverage to politics. Voters could also monitor the activities of those serving in government themselves. There is all kinds of information about Congress online (e.g., roll call votes, interest group ratings, measures of productivity, the text of legislation, campaign finance reports, etc.). Many of the activities that members of Congress are engaged in can be monitored using preexisting sources.

Notes

1. http://www.gallup.com/poll/165809/congressional-approval-sinks-record-low.aspx.
2. http://fivethirtyeight.com/datalab/disliking-congress-as-a-whole-and-as-individuals/.
3. http://www.gallup.com/poll/162362/americans-down-congress-own-representative.aspx.
4. http://www.sciencedirect.com/science/article/pii/S0261379414000134 and http://faculty.ucmerced.edu/jtrounstine/Trounstine_LSQ.pdf.
5. http://www.nationaljournal.com/congress/if-voters-hate-congress-so-much-then-why-hasn-t-any-incumbent-lost-a-primary-20140521.
6. http://www.pearsonhighered.com/educator/product/Politics-of-Congressional-Elections-The-8E/9780205251766.page.
7. https://www.opensecrets.org/bigpicture/pac2cands.php?cycle=2012&display=.
8. http://www.opensecrets.org/news/2010/09/many-house-incumbents-heavily-relying-on-pac-cash/.
9. http://www.opensecrets.org/news/2010/09/many-house-incumbents-heavily-relying-on-pac-cash/.
10. http://www.ajc.com/news/news/local/pacs-stick-with-incumbents/nQg3H/.
11. https://www.press.umich.edu/pdf/0472099213-ch8.pdf.
12. https://sites.sas.upenn.edu/sites/default/files/jdarr/files/darr_-_the_news_you_use.pdf.
13. http://www.huffingtonpost.com/2014/06/29/incumbents-reelection_n_5541055.html.
14. http://www.nationaljournal.com/congress/if-voters-hate-congress-so-much-then-why-hasn-t-any-incumbent-lost-a-primary-20140521.
15. http://fivethirtyeight.com/datalab/disliking-congress-as-a-whole-and-as-individuals/.
16. http://voteview.com/blog/?p=726; http://www.washingtonpost.com/blogs/monkey-cage/wp/2014/02/13/polarization-in-congress-has-risen-sharply-where-is-it-going-next/.
17. http://voteview.com/blog/?p=726.
18. http://www.washingtonpost.com/blogs/monkey-cage/wp/2014/01/13/how-political-polarization-creates-stalemate-and-undermines-lawmaking/.
19. http://faculty.georgetown.edu/hcn4/Downloads/BMN_APR2012.PDF.
20. http://www.mischiefsoffaction.com/2014/05/polarization-is-not-about-legislatures.html.
21. https://rooneycenter.nd.edu/assets/12143/conflictext_activists_ms25.pdf.
22. Ibid.
23. http://faculty.georgetown.edu/hcn4/Downloads/BMN_APR2012.PDF.
24. Ibid.
25. http://themonkeycage.org/2012/05/15/polarization-is-real-and-asymmetric/.
26. http://www.cbsnews.com/news/tea-party-supporters-who-they-are-and-what-they-believe/.
27. https://www.apsanet.org/imgtest/voicememo.pdf.
28. http://press.uchicago.edu/ucp/books/book/chicago/T/bo16956602.html.
29. http://www.washingtonpost.com/opinions/hate-our-polarized-politics-why-you-cant-blame-gerrymandering/2012/10/26/c2794552-1d80-11e2-9cd5-b55c38388962_story.html.

30. http://voteview.com/ajps_393.pdf.
31. Bafumi, Joseph, and Michael Herron. 2010. "Leapfrog Representation and Extremism: A Study of American Voters and Their Members in Congress." *American Political Science Review* 104: 519–542.
32. http://blogs.lse.ac.uk/usappblog/2014/07/30/political-polarization-discourages-moderate-state-legislators-from-running-for-congress-making-the-problem-worse/.
33. http://blogs.lse.ac.uk/usappblog/2014/07/30/political-polarization-discourages-moderate-state-legislators-from-running-for-congress-making-the-problem-worse/.
34. https://www.law.berkeley.edu/files/ch_6_segura_woods_3-9-07.pdf.
35. Bafumi, Joseph, Robert Erikson, and Christopher Wlezien. 2010. "Balancing, Generic Polls, and Midterm Congressional Elections." *Journal of Politics* 72: 705–719.
36. http://leg.mt.gov/content/Committees/Interim/2011-2012/Districting/Other-Documents/REVISED%20Redistricting%20Op-Ed.pdf.
37. Panagopoulos, Costas. 2013. "Public Awareness and Attitudes about Redistricting Reform." *Journal of Politics and Law* 6: 45–54.
38. http://wedrawthelines.ca.gov/commission.html.
39. http://www.psmag.com/politics-and-law/want-reduce-polarization-improve-journalism-65003.

6

STATE AND LOCAL ELECTIONS

We start with a confession: One of us (we won't disclose which), growing up in the early 1980s, can remember spending Saturday afternoons watching a hulking guy wearing a T-shirt emblazoned with the motto "Win if you can, lose if you must, but always cheat!" pulverize his opponents in the wrestling arena. Perhaps the motto should have been a harbinger of a political career to come, but that seemed like a stretch at the time. But in 1991, that man was sworn in as mayor of Brooklyn Park, Minnesota, and eight years after that, Jesse "The Body" Ventura became the thirty-eighth governor of the state.

Glitzy national elections for president or even members of Congress often take center stage during election years, but as we note in Chapter 2, the lion's share of elections in the United States takes place in states, counties, and municipalities across the country. Voters select governors, state legislators, and other statewide officials at regular intervals every few years, but they are also asked to cast ballots for city councilors, town selectmen, school board members, judges, mayors, and the proverbial dogcatchers in nearly endless fashion. In many states, voters also chime in on policy questions at the ballot box via initiatives or referenda. These elections are an integral part of democracy in America. While it is beyond the scope of this volume to present a comprehensive overview of the structural features of each of these kinds of races, our discussion of electoral politics would be incomplete without at least some discussion of local elections.

A Brief Overview of State and Local Elections

Races for governor in states across the county tend to be the most high-profile elections below the national level. In all but two states, governors serve four-year terms, and their election takes place in a staggered manner but typically at the same time as federal elections. In five states—Kentucky,

Louisiana, Mississippi, New Jersey, and Virginia—elections for state offices are held in off-years, when no federal elections are generally scheduled. Governors in Vermont and New Hampshire are elected biennially, serving two-year terms. Gubernatorial elections (the technical term for governors' races) are typically high-salience affairs that tend to attract experienced or high-profile candidates (e.g., Jesse Ventura, Arnold Schwarzenegger, etc.) and relatively large numbers of voters, although participation in these races is generally higher when they occur in conjunction with federal races. In many ways, gubernatorial elections are not dissimilar from federal elections, with candidates competing within parties for nominations and mounting sophisticated, professional, and expensive campaigns. Since 1980, total spending on gubernatorial elections has more than doubled, with over $1.1 billion spent on these elections throughout America in the 2008 cycle alone.[1] While vote choices in gubernatorial elections can be driven by statewide factors (like the performance of the state's economy), national forces including the national economy and perceptions about the incumbent president or party also influence outcomes.

Similarly, candidates running for other statewide offices (state treasurer, attorney general, secretary of state) or legislative seats in states across the country are not immune from national forces. Like federal and statewide elections, state legislative campaigns have also become increasingly professionalized—and costly—over the past few decades, with many of the patterns detected in national elections now characterizing state legislative races as well. Incumbency advantage is just as powerful a force in state legislative races as it is in congressional elections. In the 2012 cycle, for instance, incumbents seeking reelection raised more than twice as much money as all other candidates and were successful in more than nine in ten races.[2] In many cases, competition was scarce. In fact, one-third of seats up for election in the 2012 cycle were not even contested.

There are also some important differences between national and sub-national elections. Governors in 36 states and state legislators in 15 states are subject to limits to the number of terms they can serve. A list of the current states with terms limits is shown in Table 6.1. Term limits became a popular reform movement in the 1990s, partly in response to declining competitiveness and to the perception that elected officials were becoming increasingly unaccountable and disconnected from average citizens. Term limits were adopted to address these concerns, but the evidence to date suggests they may not be very effective in doing so.[3] Instead, one report noted, "Term limited legislatures report more general chaos, a decline in civility, reduced influence of legislative leaders

94

and committees, and in some states, a shift in power relationships."[4] At the federal level, term limits have been proposed but never adopted for members of Congress, while the Twenty-Second Amendment restricts U.S. presidents to two terms in the White House. Another distinction between the national and states levels is that congressional representatives are selected in single-member districts (distinct geographical districts/constituencies that only elect one representative), while state legislative chambers in 10 states have multimember districts in which electoral districts send two or more members to legislative bodies.

Low and declining competition and participation rates, with growing professionalization and expenses, are features of many local elections as well. As a result, incumbents enjoy advantages in races for mayor, city or town council, county-wide offices, school boards, and hundreds of other offices to which citizens elect public officials across the country. Many local elections, including mayoral elections in five of the country's most populous cities (New York City, Los Angeles, Chicago, Houston, and Philadelphia), take place in off-year cycles. In many such races, the potency of partisan attachments is unavailable to candidates because elections are nonpartisan, with no party affiliations appearing on ballots.

Table 6.1 States with Terms Limits (2015)

States with Term Limits for House and/ or Senate	States with Term Limits for Governor		
Arizona	Alabama	Maryland	Pennsylvania
Arkansas	Alaska	Michigan	Rhode Island
California	Arizona	Mississippi	South Carolina
Colorado	Arkansas	Missouri	South Dakota
Florida	California	Michigan	Tennessee
Louisiana	Colorado	Montana	West Virginia
Maine	Delaware	Nebraska	Wyoming
Michigan	Florida	Nevada	
Missouri	Georgia	New Jersey	
Montana	Hawaii	New Mexico	
Nebraska	Indiana	Missouri	
Nevada	Kansas	North Carolina	
Ohio	Kentucky	Ohio	
Oklahoma	Louisiana	Oklahoma	
South Dakota	Maine	Oregon	

Note: Data from http://www.ncsl.org/research/about-state-legislatures/chart-of-term-limits-states.aspx *and* http://ballotpedia.org/States_with_gubernatorial_term_limits.

95

Voting for Judges?

Another class of officials—judges and justices—are subject to election in 39 states across the country. In some states, judicial elections for judges or state supreme court justices are partisan affairs, with party labels featured on ballots and during campaigns, while others are nonpartisan. Despite their importance, judicial elections can also feature little competition and unfold below the radar, with average voters barely aware they are going on. Even if they appear on the same ballot, voters armed with little information about these "down-ballot" races (including local, judicial, county, or other low-profile races) often just skip them, leaving them blank and resulting in what is called "roll off," or far lower numbers of votes as the ballot stretches out to lesser races. Nevertheless, judicial elections are rarely ignored by special interests or other players potentially vested in the results. These races have become increasingly expensive and professionalized and look very different from how they did in the past. Political scientist Matthew Streb argues that judicial elections have changed more than any other type of American elections in recent years.[5] Between 1990 and 2004, average spending in a contested state supreme court race nearly tripled, to almost $900,000, and the upward trend continues.[6] Total estimated spending on judicial races in the 2011–2012 cycle topped $56 million, with a record-setting $33.7 million spent on television advertisements for high court races.[7] Independent spending by well-known outside groups on both the left and the right, including Americans for Prosperity, American Votes, and the National Rifle Association, has become increasingly common in judicial races across the country. These developments have raised concerns about the integrity of the judicial process and doubts about judicial impartiality in the face of the growing need for campaign contributions. Scholarly studies have not found direct evidence that judges are affected by campaign spending, but perceptions of fairness would erode if citizens believe judges are influenced by contributions. Americans—along with more than one-in-four state judges themselves—generally believe campaign contributions influence judicial decision making.[8]

Institutional Differences Among States

Across the constellation of America's 50 states, 3,144 counties (or county equivalents like parishes in Louisiana), and 35,000 cities, towns, and villages, a range of other electoral features varies widely. Ballot access rules can be very different from place to place, governing how candidates, including federal (presidential and congressional) candidates and even political parties, get on (and stay on) ballots in various districts. These rules may include party endorsements, filing fees, age, residency, and signature requirements for candidates. Even electoral performance can be linked to ballot access for minor parties. These requirements can often be restrictive, impeding major and minor candidates from entering elections.[9] In Alabama, for example, a new party or a statewide independent candidate (for all offices except the president) needs to submit a petition with signatures totaling at least 3% of the last gubernatorial vote; if a party does get on the ballot, it needs to obtain 20% of the vote in any statewide office to stay on in subsequent races. No party or individual has managed to complete this petition since it came into existence in 1997 except the Libertarians in 2000. By contrast, Florida has no signature requirements for any type of candidate except independent presidential hopefuls.

Requirements can also vary within states by office. In New York, governors must be 30 years old and have been a resident of the state in the 5 years immediately preceding the election; state senators and state assembly members must be 18 years of age, residents of the state for 5 years, and residents of the district for 12 months immediately preceding election. The minimum number of signatures required is either 5% of the enrolled voters in the political unit or 1,250 for any congressional district, 1,000 for any state senate district, 500 for any state assembly district, 900 in any New York City council district, and 500 in any city or county legislative district outside of New York City.[10] By contrast, in Wisconsin, governors must merely be a U.S. citizen, 18 years of age or older, and have resided in the state for at least 28 consecutive days before the election, while state representatives must be state residents for at least a year as well as meeting the age and citizenship requirements at the time of taking office.

Even voting systems can vary vastly. In New York City, it is not enough for mayoral candidates competing in party primaries to get the most votes, winning by plurality; if candidates fail to attain at least 40% of the vote, the top two vote getters compete in a subsequent runoff election to determine the nominee. Similar provisions are in place even for congressional candidates and even in general elections in states like Georgia and Louisiana. In Georgia, runoff elections are held if congressional contenders fail to achieve a majority (50% plus one vote) in the general election. While plurality rules are in place in the vast majority of jurisdictions, voting systems that impose thresholds like these are commonplace. Still other localities, like San Francisco, Berkeley, and Oakland, California, and jurisdictions in at least ten states since 2012 have adopted instant-runoff voting (IVR) in elections. IVR simulates majority runoff elections in a single round of voting by allowing voters to rank candidates in order of choice rather than just registering their top preferences (as we typically do on ballots in elections).

States, counties, and municipalities also decide how long poll locations are open on Election Day, the deadlines and procedures for voter registration, whether voters can vote by mail or request no-fault absentee ballots, what types of voting equipment will be used, and all sorts of other details that can make the electoral process quite different as one crisscrosses this country.

There is significant variation in the administration of elections, including how state and local election administrators are selected. In some places, administrators are partisan and in other places there are nonpartisan election officials.[11] There are important concerns about having partisan election officials. As one study points out, "Because elections are by nature 'political,' the discretion inherent in running an election may affect whether some people are able to cast a vote—and partisan bias on the part of a local official could disadvantage some voters."[12] In recent elections, there have been major concerns about election administration. For instance, during the 2004 election, Ohio Secretary of State Kenneth Blackwell was a co-chair of President Bush's reelection campaign and made a number of controversial choices about voting procedures in Ohio, including only allowing voter registration applications to be accepted if they were on a certain weight of paper. In 2000, Florida's Secretary of State Katherine Harris co-chaired Bush's campaign and was accused of making decisions that were favorable to Bush's election campaign.

Interestingly, following the 2000 election (which generated considerable controversy about the voting process and election outcome), Congress developed and passed (in 2002) the Help America Vote Act (HAVA). This act created the Election Assistance Commission (EAC), an independent agency of the government that helps administer federal elections, designed to help states and localities move from punch card to lever-based voting systems and to establish basic standards for election administration. Although HAVA requires that states and localities update their election processes (e.g., voting machines, poll worker training, registration processes, etc.), each state has the discretion on how to implement the updates, so there has been variation in how states have interpreted the requirements and in how they have implemented reforms.

Direct Democracy

Beyond candidate elections, voters in 27 states and the District of Columbia can participate directly in public policy creation by voting on ballot initiatives or referenda. These are examples of direct democracy that enable citizens to collect signatures on petitions in order to place policy measures on ballots for direct public ratification or rejection, effectively circumventing state legislatures and often forcing the issue on hot-button controversies that legislators are reluctant to grapple with in formal governing bodies. Popularized by the Progressive era reforms of the early 1900s, voters in more than half of the country routinely decide public policy questions that can range from banning income taxes to same-sex marriage to medical marijuana use. Virtually any issue is an eligible candidate for direct democracy in permissive states. In the 2014 cycle, women's health, the minimum wage, and gun violence prevention measures were among the many policy items featured at the ballot box.

The rules governing how measures like these can end up on ballots (e.g., signature requirements, timing) differ widely across jurisdictions, but there are some trends common to ballot measures nationwide. In what is now a common refrain, campaigns for and against ballot measures are becoming increasingly sophisticated. Campaigns are now devised and executed using approaches similar to candidate elections in terms of strategy and communications. Spending on direct democracy has skyrocketed in recent years, with $1 billion spent on ballot initiatives in 11 states alone in 2012.[13] The growth in the number of policy decisions subjected to direct public input alarms some observers who wonder whether average citizens are properly equipped to render decisions on complex policy matters and whether outcomes go to the highest bidder. Oftentimes, ballot measures are worded in ways that are confusing, or even misleading, to ordinary voters. Some jurisdictions that permit direct democracy provide explanations directly on the ballot or in mailings, voter guides, or websites available to citizens in advance of the elections. Others question whether direct democracy compromises the American system of representative democracy in which voters elect legislators to promote their interests in legislative bodies. Supporters of direct democracy relish the recent developments advancing its status in American politics. In fact, some believe technological advancements like the Internet can help to promote direct democracy and to facilitate even greater direct public involvement in policy decisions.

Ways to Improve State and Local Elections

The following are some ideas on how state and local elections in the United States could be improved.

- As we noted above, many state and local elections are low-salience events. Potential voters often do not even know that these elections are happening. This suggests that efforts must be taken to increase public knowledge of when local elections are and what is at stake. There are numerous things that could be done to make citizens aware of when elections are happening, including sending reminders to vote or devoting local media attention to elections. Governments, nonprofits interested in civic engagement, or other groups at the state and local levels could do these kinds of activities. In one city in Sweden, a commission developed "Democracy Passports" that described the political powers that "citizens have and all the forums where they have the right to weigh in—at the city, state, country and European Union level. The passport explains which levels of government do what, as well as what you can do to influence the government."[14] Perhaps groups could do something like this in the United States.
- As we mentioned in Chapter 2, it would likely be helpful to move off-cycle state and local elections to times when more high-profile elections are occurring (congressional midterm or presidential, for example). Cities that have moved their local elections to presidential years have seen large increases in turnout (usually about a 20% increase but sometimes as high as 50%).[15]
- Los Angeles, California, has been experiencing low voter turnout in city council elections for some time now. One potential idea being considered in that city is to "let people cast their ballots wherever they want. Eliminate the precinct voting model and put voting centers in highly visible, well-traveled locations, such as malls or schools."[16] This could be done in other places as well if it improves turnout levels in city elections.
- Surveys have illustrated that voters prefer nonpartisan to partisan election administration (66% of people in a recent survey said they preferred nonpartisan administration and only 19.9% said they preferred partisan).[17] Studies have also demonstrated that the interaction between the partisanship of election officials and the partisanship of the electorate they are serving can influence things like voter turnout levels.[18] If citizens are concerned about election

administration, they must urge political leaders to adopt reforms that will improve the process. For instance, citizens could push for the move from partisan to nonpartisan election administration.

- Studies have demonstrated that ballot initiatives increase voter turnout.[19] If citizens are drawn to the ballot box because of direct democracy, more states and localities could consider allowing ballot initiatives. This might require that citizens push state or local governments to alter their electoral rules.

Notes

1. http://knowledgecenter.csg.org/kc/system/files/BeyleFigureA.pdf.
2. http://www.followthemoney.org/research/institute-reports/the-role-of-money-and-incumbency-in-2011-and-2012-state-legislative-races/.
3. Masket, Seth, and J. Lewis. 2007. "A Return to Normalcy? Revisiting the Effects of Term Limits on Competitiveness and Spending in California Assembly WElections." *State Politics and Policy Quarterly* 7 (1): 20–38.
4. http://www.csg.org/knowledgecenter/docs/BOS2005-LegislativeTermLimits.pdf.
5. Streb, Matthew, ed. 2007. *Running for Judge: The Rising Political, Financial and Legal Stakes of Judicial Elections*. New York, NY: New York University Press.
6. Bonneau, Chris. 2007. "The Dynamics of Campaign Spending in State Supreme Court Elections." In Streb, Matthew, ed. 2007. *Running for Judge: The Rising Political, Financial and Legal Stakes of Judicial Elections*. New York, NY: New York University Press.
7. http://newpoliticsreport.org/content/uploads/JAS-NewPolitics2012-Online.pdf.
8. Bonneau, Chris. 2007. "The Dynamics of Campaign Spending in State Supreme Court Elections." In Streb, Matthew, ed. 2007. *Running for Judge: The Rising Political, Financial and Legal Stakes of Judicial Elections*. New York, NY: New York University Press.
9. Stratmann, Thomas. 2005. "Ballot Access Restrictions and Candidate Entry in Elections." *European Journal of Political Economy* 21 (1): 59–71.
10. http://www.elections.ny.gov/NYSBOE/download/law/2014RunningForElective Office.pdf. The requirements are different for independent petitions.
11. For a tally of the different methods, see this report: http://cppa.utah.edu/_documents/publications/elections/election-governance-report.pdf.
12. https://www.supportthevoter.gov/files/2013/08/Election-Law-Journal-Helping-American-Vote.pdf.
13. http://www.washingtonpost.com/blogs/govbeat/wp/2013/11/08/initiative-spending-booms-past-1-billion-as-corporations-sponsor-their-own-proposals/.
14. http://time.com/3558705/boost-voter-turnout-sweden-america/.
15. Holbrook, Thomas, and Aaron Weinschenk. "Campaigns, Mobilization, and Turnout in Mayoral Elections." *Political Research Quarterly* 67: 42–55.
16. http://www.latimes.com/opinion/editorials/la-ed-voter-turnout-20140822-story.html.
17. Alvarez, R. Michael, and Thad Hall. 2005. "Public Attitudes About Election Governance." University of Utah Center for Public Policy and Administration and

the Caltech/MIT Voting Technology Project. http://cppa.utah.edu/_documents/publications/elections/election-governance-report.pdf.
18. Burden, Barry, David Canon, Stephane Lavertu, Kenneth Mayer, and Donald Moynihan. 2013. "Selection Method, Partisanship, and the Administration of Elections." *American Politics Research* 41: 903–936.
19. Tolbert, Caroline, John Grummel, and Daniel Smith. 2001. "The Effects of Ballot Initiatives on Voter Turnout in the American States." *American Politics Research* 29: 625–648.

7

POLITICAL PARTIES

Political parties play a central role in American political life, but citizens rarely stop to think about what a political party is. In the most obvious sense they are organizations that sponsor candidates, with the goal of controlling political offices and public policies. But parties encompass a wide range of actors in addition to the politicians serving in government or candidates running for office. One description of parties from the well-known political scientist V.O. Key suggests that there are actually three components of political parties: the party-in-electorate, the party-as-organization, and the party-in-government. The party-in-electorate refers to citizens who identify with parties. To be clear, people need not formally register with a political party in order to belong to it. Indeed, very few people in the United States are formally registered with a party but many consider themselves to be partisans. A psychological or emotional connection to a party can be quite powerful (which we will discuss in more detail below). The party-as-organization refers to the entities like national party committees or state and local party organizations that carry out the activities of the party. The party-in-government refers to those elected officials who are attached to political parties and pursue their policy goals. Based on this conceptualization, it is clear that parties are more than just elected officials or candidates for office. Political scientists have recently started to conceptualize parties even more broadly as *networks*—collections of "different types of actors—donors, activists, interest groups, officeholders, candidates, even some media officials—working together to advance a set of policy goals by controlling party nominations and winning elections."[1] Parties are important during the electoral process—providing a "brand name" or shared reputation for candidates—as well as during the governing phase after elections.

Public Perceptions of Parties

It is interesting to note that despite the centrality of parties in American politics, many Americans find modern political parties to be quite frustrating or unsatisfactory. Political parties have been described as "institutions Americans love to hate."[2] When asked about the major parties, many people respond quite negatively. For example, a poll of likely voters conducted in 2014 found that 53% thought that neither party in Congress is the party of the American people.[3] A 2013 poll conducted by Gallup found that 60% of Americans thought that the Democratic and Republican parties do such a poor job of representing the American people that a third major party is needed.[4] The numbers of people saying they have favorable views of the Democratic and Republican parties have also been quite low recently. A 2013 Gallup poll found that just 28% of Americans had a favorable view of the Republican Party and that 43% had a favorable view of the Democratic Party.[5] It is not too difficult to understand why Americans are unhappy with the major parties these days: There has been gridlock on many policy issues, Americans sense that there is a lack of bipartisanship in Washington, and the parties are remarkably polarized in Congress. Despite public dissatisfaction with political parties, it is hard to imagine American politics without them. The famous political scientist E.E. Schattschneider once noted, "It should be flatly stated that political parties created democracy and that modern democracy is unthinkable save in terms of political parties."[6] In this chapter, we provide an overview of the development of political parties in the United States and highlight the ideas that the Founders had about them (which did not agree with Schattschneider). We also provide an overview of the kinds of things that parties do during elections and in government. Even though many people complain about political parties, they are actually quite important in a democratic system. Finally, we end by discussing some of the objections that people have to political parties and suggest some things that might be done to improve the party system in the United States.

The Development of Political Parties

In order to understand the development of parties in American politics, it is necessary to look back into American history. Given the prominence of parties in today's political landscape, many people assume that they have always been around. This is actually not the case. In fact, many of the Founders were fearful of conflicting groups or parties emerging.

James Madison, for instance, wrote about his concerns with "factions." In Federalist No. 10, which was published in 1787, Madison stated, "By a faction, I understand a number of citizens, whether amounting to a majority or a minority of the whole, who are united and actuated by some common impulse of passion, or of interest, adverse to the rights of other citizens, or to the permanent and aggregate interests of the community. There are two methods of curing the mischiefs of faction: the one, by removing its causes; the other, by controlling its effect."[7]

George Washington was also concerned about parties, or the "mischief of factions," noting that "the alternate domination of one faction over another, sharpened by the spirit of revenge, natural to party dissension, which in different ages and countries has perpetrated the most horrid enormities, is itself a frightful despotism."[8] It often surprises people to find out that political parties are actually not mentioned in the U.S. Constitution (the Founders hoped to avoid them). The Constitution does not specify that political parties must exist (although it does enable groups to form—the Bill of Rights recognizes freedom of association, which is necessary for groups to develop and endure). Many of the Founders were concerned that parties would lead to protracted argumentation and gridlock. In addition, there was concern that parties might put their own interests ahead of the public interest. Despite the concerns about parties expressed by the Founders (and their hope to avoid them under the Constitution), political parties did emerge early on in American history (and many of the Founders who bemoaned parties were actually involved with them during their time in government). Even Madison, who expressed concern about parties in 1787, noted several years later in 1792 that "in every political society, parties are unavoidable."[9] The question for Madison was how to deal with parties and the divisions they might foster.

The first political parties emerged in the late 1790s and the United States has had parties ever since—although the party system has changed over time. Parties became important because they provided a mechanism for like-minded people to band together and express their opinions. Importantly, parties also provided a mechanism for getting people involved in the political process. The 1824 election provides an interesting example of how parties can mobilize voters. Andrew Jackson won the popular vote in that contest but not the majority of Electoral College votes. John Adams (the second-place candidate) and Henry Clay (the fourth-place candidate and Speaker of the House) struck a deal so that Adams would be declared the winner and Clay would be appointed as the secretary of state after Adams assumed his position as the president. This event sparked voter mobilization efforts by the parties. Indeed, "Party operatives spread the word that unless average citizens became involved, elite deals of this sort would be common. It was a call to the average citizen to stand up and exert his role in the political process. This emphasis on individual involvement ushered in a new era in electoral politics ... Politics *was* for the average person—not just the economic and social elite."[10] Our goal here is not to provide an in-depth overview of the development of the American party system (which has been discussed in detail in many other books) but instead to point out that parties were originally not viewed as an important or desirable feature in American politics—in fact, many people thought that they would do more harm than good. After parties emerged, however, people began to realize how valuable (and unavoidable) they were. Indeed, from the standpoint of candidates and elected officials, political parties are quite important. Political scientist John Aldrich has pointed out that parties form and endure because they serve the needs of politicians: They help regulate the number of people seeking elective office, they mobilize voters during elections, and they help create the majorities that are needed to accomplish goals once in office.[11]

What Do Parties Do?

It is easy to complain about political parties, especially during times of extreme party polarization. Pundits, journalists, and ordinary citizens do it all the time. It is important to note that, despite their flaws, political parties actually do a lot of crucial things within our political system. One is to recruit candidates to run for elective office. Local, state, and national party organizations are constantly on the lookout for political talent. Parties also help candidates by providing them with resources and organizational support during elections. Parties often provide candidates with campaign assistance and financial help. It is not uncommon for national party committees to transfer money to political candidates during elections or to help them in fundraising.[12] Interestingly, in recent years, political consultants and campaign professionals have come to play a more prominent role in campaigns, perhaps because over time parties have become less able to provide services that candidates need or want. For a fee, these political professionals provide specialized expertise and guidance about campaign messaging and targeting, media production and communications plans, fundraising, public relations, and almost every other aspect of campaign management. Parties clearly still matter, but the ways that they interact with campaigns appear to be changing. Indeed, most political scientists believe that since the 1960s, political campaigns have become increasingly "candidate-centered" rather than "party-centered." In short, the individual attributes of political candidates are now more influential than in the past and traditional party organizations have weakened.

Another important function of parties is to aggregate preferences. Parties take the political views of different individuals and groups in society and combine them into a platform or series of policy programs. Parties "bundle" different issues, attributes, and policies together and work hard to convince voters that they will do the best job representing them if elected. One interesting idea that has emerged is party issue "ownership."[13] The basic idea behind the issue of ownership is that parties have become associated with certain issues on which they are perceived as more competent. For example, voters typically associate environmental issues with the Democratic Party, tax cuts with the Republican Party, education with the Democratic Party, and national defense with the Republican Party. It makes sense that if a party is perceived to "own" an issue, it will be advantaged during elections if the issue is salient to voters at that time.

Importantly, parties provide citizens with a way of connecting to their government. In short, they provide a mechanism for political representation. Candidates run under party labels, which correspond to different policy positions, and voters expect candidates to pursue those policies once in office. Parties also provide a mechanism for political accountability. If a political party does not do what voters want, voters can vote against that party during the next election. Parties mobilize people to run for political office, but they also mobilize ordinary voters to turn out to vote during elections. Parties often organize get-out-the-vote activities, which are aimed at getting citizens to the polls on Election Day. During the past few election cycles, fairly large portions of the American electorate have reported being contacted by at least one of the two major political parties (35% in 2000, 43% in 2004, and 42% in 2008).[14] Of course, parties are also interested in mobilizing people to participate in many other political activities as well. For instance, as the costs of campaigning and advertising have increased over time, political parties have become increasingly interested in collecting campaign donations. They also actively recruit people to work on political campaigns. Related to the idea of political mobilization, parties also educate voters through their efforts. The campaign advertisements, mailers, and radio spots created by parties provide potential voters with information about the candidates. As citizens are exposed to campaign information, they become more likely to vote on Election Day.[15] Another thing that parties do is quite obvious—they help organize government. After elections are over, parties play an important role in the governing process. Indeed, parties and committees are the two most important organizing features in the U.S. Congress. Parties are also important because they provide an information shortcut that is useful to voters on Election Day. Seeing a "D" or an "R" next to candidate's name on a ballot can tell a voter a lot about what that person might do if elected (if voters understand what the parties represent).

Before we move forward, it is worth devoting a bit more attention to the impact of parties on the electorate. At the outset, we mentioned the idea of a psychological connection to political parties. In the United States, most people identify with a political party. Although few people are registered members of the party they associate with, the cognitive and emotional attachments that people have are remarkably powerful during elections. In Figure 7.1, we provide a look at the distribution of partisanship in the American electorate. The number of people who do not have an attachment to a particular party (pure independents) is quite small. In every year, the majority of the electorate identifies with one of the major political parties. Studies have consistently demonstrated that an individual's political partisanship is one of the strongest predictors of their vote choice on Election Day.[16] Decades of political science studies have shown that individual partisan attachments are quite stable over time.[17] Partisan attachments often develop early on—usually through family socialization—and endure over the course of one's life.[18] One should not take this to mean, though, that we will observe the same election outcomes over time. Indeed, party coalitions (the groups that come together to support parties) are not fixed and can change over time. Indeed, the Democratic Party used to be the dominant party in the southern part of the United States up until the civil rights era. Staring in the 1960s, the Republican Party began to pursue a more conservative electoral base and the Democratic Party began to pursue a more liberal base. In short, there was an electoral realignment in the party system. Today, the South tends to be solidly Republican and the North tends to be more Democratic when it comes to national politics.

As important as partisan identification is for voters (more on this later), some are willing to cross party lines to vote for candidates from different parties. Figure 7.2 shows the percentage of people splitting their vote in presidential and U.S. House elections over time. Although split-ticket voting was much more common in the 1970s and 1980s, there are still some people who vote for candidates of different parties for different offices. In 2008, for example, 17% of people engaged in split-ticket voting. The decline in split-ticket voting may signal that party loyalties are stronger now than in the recent past, but it is still important to note that some voters are not completely bound by partisan inclinations. In short, there may be some voters out there who are "persuadable" and who may be responsive to campaign appeals.

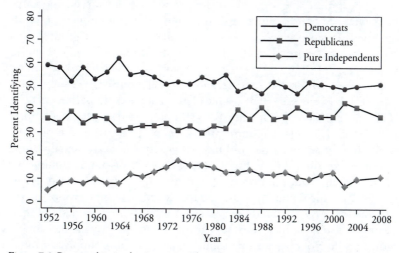

Figure 7.1 Partisanship in the American Electorate, 1952–2008. Data from American National Election Studies (http://www.electionstudies.org).

Figure 7.2 Split-Ticket Voting (Presidential and House Elections), 1952–2008. Data from American National Election Studies (http://www.electionstudies.org).

We recognize there are many other things parties do, but the discussion above provides an overview of their key functions. Even if people are not particularly fond of parties, they actually do serve a lot of important purposes in our political system. As John Aldrich has pointed out, "Democracy is *unworkable* save in terms of political parties."[19]

Before proceeding to a discussion of some of the recent developments in U.S. party politics, it is important to take a moment to point out the difference between political parties and interest groups. This is something that tends to confuse a lot of people. An interest group is simply a collection of people who want to influence public policy. Many people think that parties and interest groups are synonymous. It is certainly the case that many of the activities of parties are also things that interest groups do. For example, interest groups, like parties, mobilize voters, support candidates, and advertise. Despite the similarities between parties and interest groups, there are actually some important distinctions. Political parties care about public policy, like interest groups, but differ from interest groups in that parties run candidates for office while interest groups do not. Interest groups might support (or oppose) a candidate, but they do not run candidates of their own. It is also important to note that interest groups usually have much more specific policy goals than political parties. For example, an interest group might form to address environmental issues. Parties, however, generally take positions on a wide range of issues. This is not to say that interest groups are disconnected from parties. Quite the opposite, interest groups care a great deal about the activities and positions of parties.

Recent Developments in American Party Politics

There are some important recent developments that have shaped how people perceive parties as well as influenced the outcomes that we get out of government. One of the most interesting observations about political parties is they have become increasingly ideologically polarized over time. According to measures of the ideological locations of the Democratic and Republican parties, the distance between the parties has been growing. Figure 7.3 provides a look at the extent of political polarization over time. Higher values on the left axis indicate greater ideological distance. Clearly the parties are more ideologically distant now than ever before. Figures 7.4 and 7.5 provide a sense of how the average ideological positions of the Democratic and Republican members of both chambers in Congress have changed over time. Put simply, over the past several decades Democrats in the House and Senate have been becoming more liberal and Republicans have been becoming more conservative.

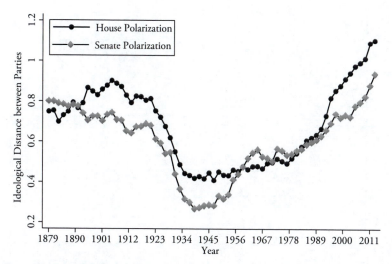

Figure 7.3 Party Polarization in U.S. Congress over Time, 1879–2011.
Data from voteview.com.

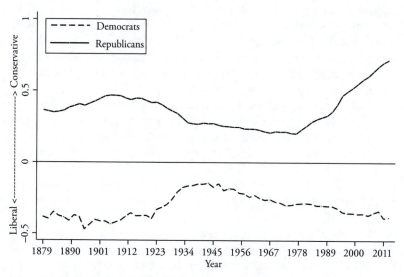

Figure 7.4 Ideological Locations of Democratic and Republican Parties, U.S. House,
1879–2011. Data from voteview.com.

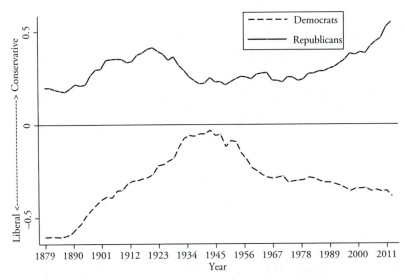

Figure 7.5 Ideological Locations of Democratic and Republican Parties, U.S. Senate, 1879–2011. Data from voteview.com.

Although many people are frustrated by current levels of partisan polarization, we note that ideological polarization in Congress is not an entirely new development (although parties seem to be divided on more issues now than in the past). In fact, polarization is actually the norm in the United States. It is certainly true, though, that the United States has experienced some periods when there was more ideological overlap between the parties. For instance, following World War II, there was broad bipartisan agreement. In fact, during the 1950s, the parties were so similar that there was concern about the parties not providing voters with real choices.[20] As we noted above, political parties are supposed to help facilitate electoral competition by providing voters with contrasting platforms and policy proposals.

The civil rights movement in the 1960s led to a shakeup of the party system and fostered ideological differences between the two major parties. Southern states were resistant to the civil rights movement and became aligned with the Republican Party, which become more conservative at that point in time. In short, the Democratic and Republican parties began to pull apart. Interestingly, cross-party voting persisted for some time in congressional elections, in part because of the "incumbency advantage" that exists in congressional elections and the "personal vote" that many members of Congress were able to cultivate.

When cross-pressured legislators began to retire or lose reelection bids in the late 1970s and 1980s, congressional elites become more polarized. Indeed, Figure 7.3 shows that party polarization in both the U.S. House and U.S. Senate started to increase steadily from the late 1970s onward. Since then, party polarization has intensified with virtually every election cycle.

How can we explain why the parties have become more polarized over time? Some scholars argue that political activists—those who are highly engaged in politics and vocal about the issues of interest to them—played an important role in stimulating parties to shift their ideologies. Since the 1960s, the major parties have made it easier to participate in party politics. Political nominations, which used to be handled by party bosses, now occur in primaries and caucuses. As a consequence, activist groups have had an easier time getting involved in and influencing the parties. But why should members of Congress be paying more attention to activists over time? Political scientist Seth Masket provides an explanation: "Activists have to offer the politicians help (in terms of labor, endorsements, or money) to make up for the politicians changing their stance in a slightly less popular way, or they have to pose a threat (depriving them of labor, endorsements, or money) if the politicians don't change their stance. Only when the reward or threat is perceived as great enough to overcome the penalty a politician believes she will face for switching to a less popular stance will a change happen." According to Masket, political activists have gotten better and better at organizing and influencing members of Congress in recent decades. He also notes that activist groups have developed around a wide range of political issues and they are continually working hard to make sure that politicians adopt the positions they prefer.[21] Research has shown that activists are much more likely than ordinary Americans to hold ideologically extreme positions.[22] If politicians are increasingly paying attention to activists, it makes sense that we would see ideological divergence. Indeed, in the contemporary Congress there are now few conservative Democrats and few liberal Republicans. There is less ideological overlap between the parties, which stands in stark contrast to earlier periods in American politics like the 1950s when there were liberals and conservatives in both parties. Perhaps unsurprisingly, given the previous discussion of the ideological extremity of activists and the strategies they use to influence members of Congress, the number of moderates serving in Congress has declined in recent decades, as Figure 7.6 illustrates. Just to be clear, the influence of activists is likely not the only factor that has influenced levels of polarization (though it certainly seems to play a key role). As we noted in Chapter 5, the idea that moderate state legislators are reluctant to run for Congress in the context of high levels of polarization also seems to play a role in fueling congressional polarization.

An alternative explanation for growing partisan polarization at the level of the political elite is rooted in the mass electorate more broadly: Politicians are more polarized because the citizenry is more polarized. On this score, there is a vibrant debate among scholars. While some find strong evidence of ideological polarization at the mass level, others are not convinced. Stanford University political scientist Morris Fiorina, for example, claims that ideological polarization in the American public is a myth. He argues Americans are closely but not deeply divided, mainly because we are often ambivalent or uncertain about making firm commitments to parties or politicians or because we are instinctively centrists or moderates in our ideological outlooks.[23] Critics, including Emory University's Alan Abramowitz, disagree. Abramowitz and his colleagues argue ideological polarization among the mass public has increased dramatically since the 1970s, and that ideological divisions are not restricted to a small minority of activists; instead, they are pervasive, involving large segments of the public. In fact, the deepest divisions are found among the most interested, informed, and active citizens.[24] Interestingly, Abramowitz and Saunders find that polarization may actually energize voters and promote political participation. While the debate about mass polarization in the electorate rages on, scholars are much less divided on the question of elite-level polarization and have focused on its consequences and implications, including party unity in legislative settings.

Let's look more closely at party unity in Congress as it relates to polarization. Often frustrating to ordinary Americans is the extent to which politicians "toe the party line." Many Americans express preferences for bipartisanship in government.[25] It is possible to get a sense of the extent to which party unity exists in both chambers of Congress. Figures 7.7 and 7.8 provide a look at party unity scores for the Democratic and Republican parties in the House and Senate over time. Party unity scores simply measure the proportion of Democrats (or Republicans) who vote with the majority of their party. The figures make it clear that party unity has always been fairly high in the United States but that it has been increasing over time. In short, there is a great deal of party loyalty within the major parties today.

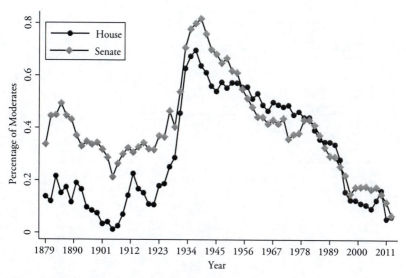

Figure 7.6 Percentage of Moderate Legislators in U.S. Congress over Time, 1879–2011. Data from voteview.com.

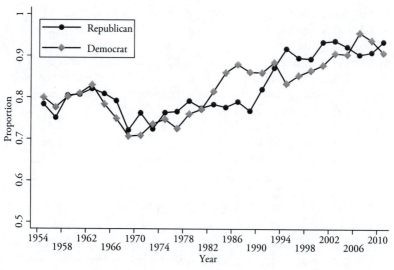

Figure 7.7 Party Unity in U.S. House, 1954–2010. Data from voteview.com.

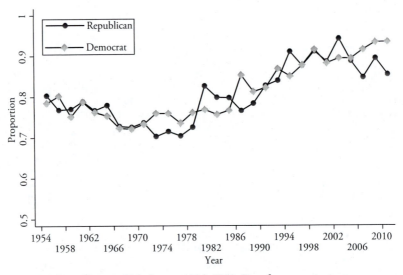

Figure 7.8 Party Unity in U.S. Senate, 1954–2010. Data from voteview.com.

Party polarization and party loyalty are often frustrating to people because they can make it difficult for the government to take action to address pressing issues. At the start of this chapter, we pointed out that ordinary Americans have been quite unhappy with the Democratic and Republican parties of late. In fact, a large majority (60% in 2013 and 58% in 2014, according to Gallup polls) has expressed a desire to see a third party emerge in U.S. politics. In part, these numbers reflect dissatisfaction with party polarization and gridlock. Despite this interest, third-party candidates typically have a hard time winning in elections. In the 2012 presidential election, for example, the Libertarian Party candidate received less than 1% of the popular vote and the Green Party candidate received 0.36% of the popular vote. If Americans are so enthusiastic about a third party, why do we see third-party candidates doing so poorly in elections?

The answer to this question is actually pretty straightforward, although most people have probably not been exposed to ideas about why the U.S. political system fosters two parties. In the 1950s, French sociologist Maurice Duverger made a number of important observations about the effects of electoral systems on political parties. He noted that plurality rule in single-member districts tends to produce two parties.[26] This is exactly the kind of system we have in the United

States. Voters get a single vote that they can cast for just one candidate in their district. Each district elects just one representative. The election winner is determined in a very simple way: The candidate who gets the most votes wins (plurality rule). This type of system tends to foster two parties for a few reasons. First, because only one candidate can win in each district, parties that take third place will not get represented in the government, regardless of their vote share. Thus, weak or small parties would likely be better off integrating into a larger party (that is closest to their ideology) in order to improve their chances of winning or to make their preferences known.[27] It is especially difficult for third parties to win seats when they are geographically dispersed. In the 1992 presidential election, for example, Ross Perot, an independent presidential candidate, won about 19% of the popular vote but did not get a single Electoral College vote. In short, his supporters weren't concentrated enough to secure victory. Second, voters tend to abandon weaker parties, instead opting to support one of the larger parties. The logic here is pretty simple and strategic. According to Duverger, if the candidate you prefer is unlikely to win (as is the case for many third-party candidates), the next best thing to do would be to vote for a second or third choice who might win (and who is closest to your original preference).[28]

According to Duverger, while plurality elections tend to produce two-party competition, proportional representation (PR) tends to favor multiple parties. Under PR, the percentage of seats that a party gets in parliament corresponds to the percentage of the vote that it received. In short, in PR systems, it is possible to win a small share of the vote and to then get a small share of the seats in the legislature. Such systems generally avoid the conditions in plurality systems that foster two parties. One thing worth noting is that a country's system of government also impacts political parties. In parliamentary systems, for example, there are more opportunities for political parties to exert influence because government emerges directly from the parliament (the chief executive is not elected separately, like a U.S. president, but is selected by the majority of the national legislature). In a presidential system like the United States, in which the president is elected (at least indirectly) by the people rather than by parliament, coalitions of different parties are less likely to form because the system provides fewer incentives for different parties to cooperate with one another in government.

We should also note that ballot access laws in the United States impact third parties. In many states, the requirements for a third party to get on the ballot are quite rigorous. For instance, a party might have to get a large number of signatures and pay a filing fee. The more difficult it is for a party to get on the ballot, the less likely it is that it will participate in elections.[29] In 2012, the Libertarian candidate and the Constitution Party candidate were on the ballot in some states but were not listed in other states. The reason for this difference is that states vary in how difficult they make it to get on the ballot. In Colorado, for example, it is quite simple—it requires a proclamation of intent and a $500 filing fee. In Oklahoma, the requirements are much different—candidates need to gather tens of thousands of signatures.[30] Given the nature of our system and the ballot access laws that exist in most states, it seems very unlikely that a viable third party will emerge in the United States, despite public interest in more political parties. Some might point to the Tea Party as a new third party, but many analysts consider this group to be more of a social movement than a political party with a formal organization or infrastructure. The Tea Party might provide endorsements for certain candidates (and certainly has a conservative ideology) but the Tea Party label hasn't appeared on any ballots. Plus, the Tea Party movement is rather decentralized—it's essentially a loose collection of different organizations, which is more characteristic of a social movement than a political party.

Although minor parties often have a hard time getting candidates elected, Americans are certainly free to vote for minor-party candidates. There are literally hundreds of registered parties across the United States, some of which have received media attention and had electoral success. For example, the Green Party of the United States has had some success getting candidates elected—mostly at the local level. The party's website lists well over 100 officeholders across the United States.[31] Of course, not all minor parties have been as successful as the Green Party. Some minor parties, like the "Rent Is Too Damn High Party," a political party in the state of New York, seem to be more humorous than anything else and are not taken very seriously by voters.

Minor parties are not a new phenomenon. The constellation of active minor or third political parties has varied widely over the course of the nation's history. For instance, President Theodore Roosevelt formed the Progressive Party of 1912 (also called the Bull Moose Party) after he was not selected as the Republican nominee. Although it has been difficult for minor or third parties to win in U.S. elections, if voters were interested in seeing more parties appear on the ballot, they could certainly pursue changes to ballot access laws. Of course, if voters coordinated to support a third-party or minor-party candidate, it would certainly be possible for such a candidate to win elective office.

Before we discuss ways to improve the party system in the United States, it is important to address one observation that has been made about political parties. Some political observers have noted that parties have become less relevant over time. There are a number of different arguments that have been made in support of this idea. For instance, during the 1970s there was an increase in the number of political independents in the United States. Many people took this to mean that the parties were becoming less important—that Americans were abandoning parties and party politics.[32] Some might also take the statistics on public dissatisfaction with the major parties presented above to mean that voters are abandoning party politics. The notion of party decline has been refuted by a number of studies in political science. Scholars have demonstrated that individual partisanship remains one of the strongest predictors of vote choice and is an even stronger predictor now than in the past.[33] If parties were becoming irrelevant, why would voters be relying on their partisanship even more when making political choices? Even people who initially say they are independents often vote consistently for one party or the other. The number of true independents in the electorate is really quite small (about 10%). It is also important to note that partisanship is now more important than ever before in Congress. The parties have staked out very different positions on many domestic issues. As one analyst noted, "Where parties in earlier periods may have found many areas of agreement even as they fought bitterly over some issues, parties today disagree on virtually everything."[34] Presumably, this disagreement exists because the people who are engaging with political parties in the United States have different preferences and want different things out of government. Given these observations, it seems a bit far-fetched to say that parties do not matter much anymore. They matter a lot! And the actions that parties take have an impact on voters as well as on the outcomes that we get out of government.

Ways to Improve the Party System

As we did in the previous chapters, we would like to end by providing some ideas on how party politics in the United States could be improved.

- Many people seem dissatisfied with having just two major parties contesting most elections. There are literally hundreds of minor parties in the United States. If citizens are interested in more party competition, it could be worthwhile to work on changing state-level ballot access requirements. Making it easier for minor-party candidates to get on the ballot would provide voters with more choices on Election Day. This would require that citizens pressure state legislators to alter ballot requirements.

- There is much concern about levels of party polarization these days. Political scientists Ray La Raja and Brian Schaffner suggest an interesting idea to decrease polarization—give political parties more money. Their argument is based on evidence that parties often mediate ideological sources of money and distribute that money to moderate candidates. Interestingly, they find that "states with 'party-centered' campaign finance laws tend to be less polarized than states that constrain how the parties can support candidates."[35] They go on to note that "unmediated financial support from donors to candidates encourages polarization" and that "limiting party organizations therefore shifts the balance of power within party coalitions away from the pragmatists toward the purists. The result is more officeholders who hold very conservative or liberal views." The implication is that changing campaign finance law to give parties more power over campaign finance could be important to reducing levels of political polarization in the United States.

- One novel idea to addressing party polarization would simply be to accept that it is going to continue. Although that does not seem like much of a solution, we could accept polarization *and* work to reform our government so that it works better with polarized parties. For instance, it may be possible to incentivize members of Congress, if we think they are too loyal to their own party, to participate in bipartisan groups or forums, which could influence their likelihood of working in a bipartisan manner. Using elections (e.g., voting people out of office) as a check on members of Congress who do not vote in bipartisan ways is one method of encouraging cooperation. The voting records for all members of Congress are available online, so voters can monitor their activities. It may also be possible to have civic organizations host bipartisan forums that bring legislators of different parties together to discuss and work on important issues. There are a number of organizations that are working to foster this kind of collaboration, including the Wisconsin Institute for Public Policy and Service, which hosts events that bring legislators of different parties together to foster bipartisanship and promote civility. During some of their events, this organization brings together prominent former members of Congress, like David Obey (D) and Tom Petri (R) to discuss the need for bipartisanship in Congress. Perhaps more of these events in states across the country would be helpful. It may also be helpful for new members of Congress to participate in such events (it may take voter encouragement to get them to attend) and to hear about the importance of bipartisanship from experienced members of Congress.

• As we noted above, what happens in primary elections can have an important impact on the candidates who move on to the general election. When political activists, who tend to be more ideologically extreme, make up a large portion of the electorate, it makes sense that candidates will be responsive to those activists. One basic thing that ordinary Americans could do to combat polarization is to participate more in primary elections, which tend to see very low turnout rates. This could potentially increase the number of moderates and independents in the electorate (these types of voters often do not participate in primary elections at high rates). There are a variety of changes that could increase voter engagement in elections, as we note in Chapter 2.

Notes

1. http://www.brookings.edu/~/media/research/files/papers/2014/03/20%20 masket/masket_mitigating%20extreme%20partisanship%20in%20an%20 era%20of%20networked%20parties.pdf.
2. White, John K., and Daniel M. Shea. 2000. *New Party Politics: From Jefferson and Hamilton to the Information Age.* New York, NY: Bedford/St. Martin's.
3. http://www.rasmussenreports.com/public_content/politics/general_politics/ april_2014/53_think_neither_political_party_represents_the_american_people.
4. http://www.gallup.com/poll/165392/perceived-need-third-party-reaches-new-high.aspx.
5. http://www.gallup.com/poll/165317/republican-party-favorability-sinks-record-low.aspx.
6. Schattschneider, E.E. 1942. *Party Government.* New York, NY: Rhinehart and Company.
7. http://people.hofstra.edu/alan_j_singer/294%20Course%20Pack/3.%20 D_I%20&%20Const/115.pdf.
8. http://avalon.law.yale.edu/18th_century/washing.asp.
9. http://press-pubs.uchicago.edu/founders/documents/v1ch15s50.html.
10. http://www.pearsonhighered.com/assets/hip/us/hip_us_pearsonhighered/ samplechapter/0205831230.pdf.
11. Aldrich, John. 2011. *Why Parties? A Second Look.* Chicago, IL: University of Chicago Press.
12. Holbrook, Thomas, and Scott McClurg. 2005. "The Mobilization of Core Supporters: Campaigns, Turnout, and Electoral Composition in United States Presidential Elections." *American Journal of Political Science* 49: 689–703.
13. Petrocik, John R. 1996. "Issue Ownership in Presidential Elections, with a 1980 Case Study." *American Journal of Political Science* 40 (3): 825–850.

14. http://www.electionstudies.org/nesguide/toptable/tab6c_1a.htm.

15. Holbrook, Thomas, and Aaron Weinschenk. 2014. "Campaigns, Mobilization, and Turnout in Mayoral Elections." *Political Research Quarterly* 67: 42–55.

16. Bafumi, J., and R. Y. Shapiro. 2009. "A New Partisan Voter." *Journal of Politics* 71 (1): 1–24.

17. Green, Donald, Bradley Palmquist, and Eric Schickler. 2002. *Partisan Hearts and Minds: Political Parties and the Social Identities of Voters.* New Haven, CT: Yale University Press.

18. Jennings, M. Kent, Laura Stoker, and Jake Bowers. 2009. "Politics across Generations: Family Transmission Reexamined." *Journal of Politics* 71: 782–799.

19. Aldrich, John. 1995. *Why Parties? The Origin and Transformation of Party Politics in America.* Chicago, IL: University of Chicago Press.

20. American Political Science Association. 1950. "A Report of the Committee on Political Parties: Toward a More Responsible Two-Party System."

21. http://www.psmag.com/navigation/politics-and-law/why-polarize-polarization-politics-state-legislature-81234/.

22. Layman, Geoffrey, Thomas Carsey, John Green, Richard Herrera, and Rosalyn Cooperman. 2010. "Activists and Conflict Extension in American Party Politics." *American Political Science Review* 104: 324–346.

23. Fiorina, Morris P., with Samuel J. Abrams and Jeremy C. Pope. 2006. *Culture War? The Myth of a Polarized America.* 2nd ed. New York, NY: Pearson Longman.

24. Abramowitz, Alan, and Kyle Saunders. 2008. "Is Polarization a Myth?" *Journal of Politics* 70: 542–555.

25. http://www.gallup.com/poll/145679/americans-strongly-desire-political-leaders-work-together.aspx.

26. Duverger, Maurice. 1954. *Political Parties: Their Organization and Activity in the Modern State.* New York, NY: Wiley. Translated by Barbara and Robert North.

27. Cox, Gary. 1997. *Making Votes Count.* New York, NY: Cambridge.

28. Duverger, Maurice. 1954. *Political Parties: Their Organization and Activity in the Modern State.* New York: Wiley. Translated by Barbara and Robert North.

29. Lem, Steve, and Conor Dowling. 2006. "Picking Their Spots: Minor Party Candidates in Gubernatorial Elections." *Political Research Quarterly* 59: 471–480.

30. http://www.usatoday.com/news/politics/story/2012-07-08/third-party-ballot-access/56098480/1.

31. http://www.gp.org/election-news/officeholders.

32. Wattenberg, Martin. 1998. *The Decline of American Political Parties, 1952–1996.* Cambridge, MA: Harvard University Press.

33. Bartels, Larry. 2000. "Partisanship and Voting Behavior, 1952–1996." *American Journal of Political Science* 44: 35–50. Weinschenk, Aaron. 2013. "Partisanship and Voting Behavior: An Update." *Presidential Studies Quarterly* 43: 607–617.

34. http://www.washingtonpost.com/blogs/monkey-cage/wp/2014/01/17/our-politics-is-polarized-on-more-issues-than-ever-before/.

35. http://www.washingtonpost.com/blogs/monkey-cage/wp/2014/07/21/want-to-reduce-polarization-give-parties-more-money/.

8

THE MEDIA

The media play an integral role in a democracy. Without political report-ing by the media, the public would likely know little about elections, politics, and political candidates. But media coverage of elections alone is insufficient to foster a well-functioning democracy. Political scien-tist Robert Dahl has argued that citizens must "have a right to seek out alternative sources of information. Moreover, alternative sources of information exist and are protected by law."[1] In a democratic system, citizens need to be able to understand political issues, they need to be able to get information from a diversity of sources, and there must be a press that is free from government control. In this chapter, we pro-vide an overview of the media habits of ordinary Americans. We then discuss the functions of the media in the United States. After doing so, we provide an overview of some of the most common complaints about the nature of media coverage during U.S. elections. Here, we focus on the widely held idea that media coverage is biased, the idea that people expose themselves to information that meshes with their political predispositions, and the idea that political campaigns focus too heavily on negativity in advertisements. We provide suggestions about how citizens can leverage technology to gain exposure to a wide variety of news coverage.

Where Americans Get News: Traditional and "New" Media

Scholars who study the media tend to divide them into "traditional" and "new" media. Traditional media refer to things like newspapers, magazines, television news, and radio news. Typically, traditional media are categorized as either print or broadcast media. New media refer to emerging sources of information, including websites, blogs, and social media outlets. Let's take a quick look at where Americans get their political information. The Pew Research Center often surveys Americans to learn about their media habits and preferences. Over time, Pew has asked representative samples of the American public how regularly they use a variety of media outlets to learn about presidential campaigns. Figure 8.1 shows the results from 1992 to 2012. It is clear that some media sources are much more popular than others. A sizeable portion of the American population uses television to learn about campaigns. Of the four sources shown in the figure, television is by far the most popular source of information. Relatively small portions of the population use radio or newspapers. It is interesting to note that newspaper circulation has been declining over time.[2] Presumably, part of the decline in newspaper circulation is related to the rise of the Internet. Many newspapers have adapted to this technological change and now offer news content online—sometimes for free and sometimes for a fee. We should point out that scholars have shown that local newspapers are a fairly important part of public life—they can influence levels of political engagement, voter turnout, and levels of political competition.[3] According to one recent study, "even a small newspaper … can make local politics more vibrant."[4] The decline of newspapers and newspaper circulation across the United States has led many political observers to express concern. One set of scholars pessimistically noted, "Ultimately, someday, the print product will be gone. And its replacement will not necessarily be the same number of local newspapers simply re-purposed into electronic formats. Because of the unbundling effect, it is at least possible that only a few major national or international newspaper 'brands' will survive in electronic form, and that local news will come to be delivered by, and attached to, a variety of other online services."[5] A 2011 study by Pew Research on how people learn about their local communities noted that newspapers were the source that people used most (or tied for most relied upon) for information about crime, taxes, local government activities, schools, local politics, local jobs, community/neighborhood events, zoning information, and local social services.[6] Thus, the decline of newspapers may be problematic for American democracy.

According to Figure 8.1, the percentage of people using the Internet as a source for political campaign news has, as expected, increased over time and most of the other sources have seen declines. Even so, only 34% percent of people reported regularly using the Internet to get information about the most recent presidential campaigns. When it comes to local politics, very small percentages of Americans use the Internet to get information. For instance, in a 2011 Pew survey, 22% of people said they rely on local newspapers to learn about local taxes, while 9% said they used TV news to learn about this issue, and 9% said they used the Internet. In that same survey, 19% of people said they use newspapers to learn about government activities, while 12% said they used TV news for this purpose, and 6% said they turn to the Internet. Finally, 17% of people said they used the local newspaper to learn about zoning and development, while 6% learned about this topic from TV news, and 4% learned about it from the Internet.[7]

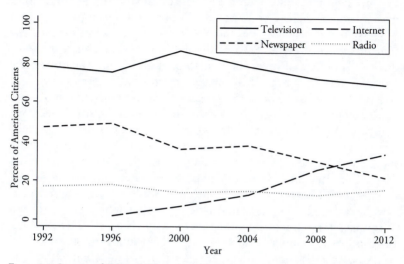

Figure 8.1 Sources of Political Campaign Information, 1992–2012. Data from Pew Research Center.

Over the past few years, one of the hottest topics has been the rise of social media platforms like Twitter and Facebook. Research has indicated that about 75% of all adults who have Internet access use social networking sites.[8] The advent of social media outlets has certainly impacted popular culture, but have social media outlets influenced how people interact with politics? Research organizations have begun asking people whether and how they use social media to learn about politics. A 2012 poll conducted by Pew Research found that 36% of social network users said that the sites were "very" or "somewhat" important in helping them keep up with political news.[9] The percentage of people who used their cell phones in 2014 to track political campaigns was 28%, and the percentage of Americans who followed candidates and other political figures on social media was 16%.[10] Given the widespread use of social media, it certainly seems likely that these outlets will continue to be a place where people can learn about and discuss elections and politics. It is worth noting that social media has become so important that many mainstream television programs and newspapers now have profiles on social media outlets where they provide information to interested citizens. The question is whether new technologies will mobilize more people to learn about and get involved in politics or if such technologies will simply reinforce preexisting media consumption and habits of participation. If it is the second (those with high propensities to engage in politics offline are the ones who engage online too), we may not see increases in overall levels of knowledge or participation.

Despite the relatively low numbers of people using some of the sources shown in Figure 8.1, we should point out that there are hundreds of sources that one could use to get political information in the United States. Over time, there has been a proliferation of media outlets, and there seems to be no turning back. There are now cable news networks, blogs, websites, web broadcasts, online magazines, and podcasts. American politics now has a true 24-hour news cycle. Today's news outlets want to be the first to cover a story, so they now add to their reporting around the clock. There are also a number of fact-checking websites that provide valuable information to potential voters and serve as a check on media outlets and political figures. In addition, many governments now have detailed political information available online. In the state of Wisconsin, for example, interested citizens can visit a website that tracks the number of hours that lobby groups spent lobbying on each piece of proposed legislation. The Federal Election Commission (FEC) and many states and localities now have fairly advanced websites that track campaign donations and expenditures. In short, potential voters can get a great deal of information about government and politics directly (without having it filtered through the media). New technologies have helped to make government processes and politics more transparent than ever before. Although many people do not seek out such information, a great deal of information is available at people's fingertips.

Functions of the Media

With the ways Americans use different media in mind, we can consider the functions of the media in a democracy. We divide these functions into five categories: *agenda-setting, framing the news, serving as a watchdog, educating the public,* and *serving as a public representative.* One of the primary roles that the media play is to set the agenda. In other words, the media, by deciding what information or news to cover, shape what people pay attention to. If the media devote attention to a particular issue or event, people will be more likely perceive it to be important. In general, people are not well informed about politics and they rely on the media to highlight important concerns. In the context of presidential campaigns, scholars have demonstrated that the media play an important role in shaping what voters consider to be the major campaign issues.[11] Because of their ability to set the agenda, media outlets have a great deal of power in American democracy, especially during election times. One scholar has noted that the press is "stunningly successful in telling its readers what to think about."[12]

The media also play a role in shaping how people interpret candidates, issues, or events, which is known as *framing*. The media can shape citizens' perceptions in different ways by making certain language choices or by providing some pieces of contextual information rather than others. It is amazing how powerful different frames can be. One recent example nicely illustrates how language can influence public perceptions of government and politics. In 2010, President Obama signed the Patient Protection and Affordable Care Act into law. The law has stimulated a great deal of controversy among politicians and ordinary citizens alike. Interestingly, research has shown that the name used to describe the act influences perceptions of it. A recent CNN poll, for example, illustrated that 46% of people opposed the act when it was called "Obamacare," a name given to the healthcare law by Republicans as a way of criticizing it, while only 37% of people opposed the proposal when it was called the "Affordable Care Act."[13] Another good example is the framing of the inheritance tax as the "death tax," which shifts the emotional reaction that people have to the tax. It appears that the language used to describe the law elicits different reactions from people. This sort of framing strongly influences public perceptions of government and politics. It's not hard to see why candidates and politicians might care about framing. If there is a frame that elicits negative perceptions from the public, it could be valuable to make that frame stick to an opposing candidate or party. If there is a frame that elicits a positive reaction from the public, a politician or candidate will want to reinforce that frame when discussing issues, developing campaign messages, and talking to members of the press.

Another role of the media is to serve as a watchdog. Journalists and reporters are supposed to act as stand-ins for ordinary citizens and provide information on events, issues, current politicians, or hopeful candidates that might be important for the public to know. After all, in order to hold politicians accountable, people need to have accurate information about what they have been doing. The public is often most concerned about abuses of power, scandals, and unethical activities. Of course, during political campaigns, voters are often interested in learning about whether the candidates' previous activities illustrate whether they are suitable for public office. The public should know if politicians or political candidates have engaged in wrongdoing. Of course, what is perceived as a scandal is heavily influenced by the media framing described above. For example, Bill Clinton's behavior in regard to Monica Lewinsky, George W. Bush's descriptions of weapons of mass destruction in Iraq, or Hillary Clinton's use of nongovernment email can all be seen as scandalous or not depending on how they are framed.

In addition to influencing what people pay attention to and serving as a watchdog, the media play an important role in educating the public. Because many voters are not able or willing to attend events like candidate debates, forums, or rallies, it makes sense that they would use the media to get information about political candidates. Thus, the media should provide a forum where ordinary citizens can learn about the differences between political candidates and parties. As Figure 8.1 showed, Americans rely quite heavily on television broadcasts to get this information. One potential limitation of relying too heavily on television coverage, though, is the tendency in television broadcasts to reduce tremendously complicated political issues down to "sound bites." In short, many media outlets will report on very complicated topics for just a few seconds. This may lead people to believe that things are simpler than they actually are in reality. There is also a tendency to focus election coverage disproportionately on the "horse race" (which candidate is ahead or behind in the polls) rather than on substantive policy issues. Of course, people do not have to rely only on the sound bite coverage typically provided by television and radio outlets to get information about politics. After being provided some basic political information, citizens could certainly turn to other sources to learn more. Indeed, in today's society there are many websites that provide in-depth analyses of government policies, candidate positions, and political issues. The problem is not that information is unavailable but that many people are not interested enough in politics.

Interestingly, political information in newspapers seems to be more informative for potential voters than information provided on television—perhaps because newspapers are often able to provide more depth than television broadcasts.[14] Of course, given that only a small portion of the population uses newspapers to get information about politics (see Figure 8.1), there are limits to the impact that newspapers can have in stimulating political learning. Perhaps more importantly, political learning does not just include acquiring factual information about politics, but also includes updating political preferences in light of new information. One critical time when political learning occurs is during presidential nominating conventions. During the conventions, the media provide comprehensive coverage of the events. Political scientists have repeatedly shown that media coverage of the conventions leads to a "convention bump," or increase in support, for candidates.[15] Thus by covering important political events, media can shape what people know about politics and the preferences they have about different candidates.

We should highlight the role that the mass media can play in stimulating political participation and in improving civic education. Political scientists Donald Green and Alan Gerber note that radio, television, and newspaper messages that encourage people to vote (or that draw attention to the idea of voting as a social norm) can increase levels of voter turnout in national and local elections—sometimes by several percentage points.[16] In addition, providing people with a newspaper subscription appears to slightly increase voter turnout.[17] Although the media provide voters with information about candidates and parties, media outlets can also be a place where people receive encouragement to participate in political life. In addition, the news media play an important role in providing information about citizens' preferences during elections. One way that they do this is by sponsoring exit polls. Exit polls are simply surveys administered immediately after voters leave their polling places on Election Day. Exit polls ask voters about their candidate choices and usually include other questions about their concerns or opinions on current issues. During national elections, the Voter News Service, a group of news media organizations—ABC, CBS, NBC, CNN, Fox, and the Associated Press—conducts exit polls so that the election results can be reported as quickly as possible. Exit polls help inform voters about the likely outcome on Election Day and have also been a valuable source of information about the electorate. Exit polls have been conducted since the 1970s and can provide a sense of electoral trends over time and insights into what factors influence vote choices.

It is also possible to think of the media as a public representative. In other words, it may be important for the media to serve as a spokesperson or advocate for the public. This could take a number of different forms. For example, it could be the case that journalists represent the public while investigating problems or scandals. Since ordinary citizens are unlikely to be able to directly ask politicians or candidates the questions they are curious about, they have to rely on the media to do so for them. Citizens should be able to get answers to the questions that interest them regarding politics. Again, in order to achieve political accountability, citizens need to have good information. One concern about the potential of the media to serve as a public representative is that the media is often interested in presenting dramatic or emotional events. After all, most media outlets are businesses and are interested in attracting and maintaining customers. Thus, there is some incentive to report on news stories that are exciting and that capture attention. This is why the media often focus on "horse race" coverage of political campaigns. If the media can make an election seem exciting or competitive, it may be possible to cultivate a larger audience. By focusing on every campaign event and poll, though, the media may create the perception that an election is more competitive than it really is.

Concerns About Media Coverage

Although most people recognize that the media is important in a democracy, one idea that many people seem to have these days is that the press is quite biased. It is imperative that citizens in a democracy are able to get information that is impartial and accurate. For many Americans, the kind of bias that is most troubling is one toward a particular ideology or party. It is interesting to note that 77% of Americans said that the media "tend to favor one side" in a 2011 poll conducted by Pew Research.[18] In another Pew poll from January 2012, 67% of people said that there is a "great deal" or a "fair amount" of political bias in news coverage. But what does political science research suggest about biases in the media? Although people often perceive that biases exist, it is interesting to note that one recent comprehensive study, which conducted an analysis of 99 previous studies of media coverage during presidential elections, found that "coverage has no aggregate partisan bias either way, even though there are small biases in specific realms that are generally insubstantial."[19] Another study on partisan media bias during presidential campaigns noted "no significant biases were found for the newspaper industry. Biases in newsmagazines were virtually zero as well. However, meta-analysis of studies of television network news showed small, measurable, but probably insubstantial coverage and statement biases."[20]

If there is little evidence of bias in media coverage, why do so many people think the media is so biased? There are a few potential reasons. One reason is that there are some news outlets that are explicitly ideological or partisan in nature. Many cable news networks (e.g., Fox News, MSNBC) devote a great deal of their programming to commentary and opinion, which often becomes openly ideological.[21] It is important to keep in mind, though, that cable news networks are not the only media outlets doing political reporting. People may infer that all media outlets are presenting information from an ideological or partisan perspective simply because they see partisan or ideological content in cable news shows. Some news sources like NewsHour on PBS tend to be quite centrist and present a range of perspectives on different issues. Another potential reason is that people tend to believe that the media outlets they use are fair and that other media outlets are biased. Indeed, when Pew asked people about the accuracy of news organizations they use the most, just 30% of people said that stories were often inaccurate. A much higher percentage (66%) said that news organizations in general often report stories that are inaccurate.[22] A final reason why the public may perceive biases in media reporting is that politics has become more ideologically polarized in recent years and people may believe that ideology is seeping into the media as well. It is interesting to note that "liberals and conservatives can (and often do) believe the same news report is biased against both their views."[23] Because ideology and partisanship have become heightened in recent years, it is not all that surprising that ideology and partisanship play a role in perceptions of the media. In 1985, 53% of people said that press coverage tends to favor one side. By 2011, that number had jumped to 77%. Despite public perceptions about media biases, academic research has illustrated that, on average, media coverage tends to be fairly balanced. Recent research has shown that people across the partisan spectrum want political news from sources that do not have political opinions. A 2012 poll conducted by Pew, for example, showed that 65% of Republicans, 71% of Democrats, and 71% of Independents want news from sources that do not have a political point of view. Despite research suggesting fairly limited media biases, people still seem to perceive significant biases in media coverage.

Although partisan or ideological biases in media coverage may not be as large as people initially suspect, we should point out that studies have illustrated that there can be biases in news coverage beyond just partisan or ideological ones. In an analysis of news coverage of U.S. House elections, political scientist Brian Schaffner found that "local news coverage is produced in a way that tends to favor incumbents."[24] Political scientists have shown that incumbents have a variety of political advantages (e.g., fundraising and name recognition) and they apparently also have advantages when it comes to news coverage. Schaffner also found evidence that "in areas where local newspapers devote more coverage to a House member, citizens are more likely to say that the incumbent is doing a good job of keeping in touch with the district and are more likely to vote for that incumbent."[25] It makes sense that if people are exposed to a great deal of information about incumbents (and information that is typically favorable to them), they would tend to view them positively.

Another idea that has captured some attention recently is the notion that people only expose themselves to news coverage and information that match their partisan or ideological leanings. In other words, liberals only look at liberal news and conservatives only look at conservative news. This is something called "selective exposure," or seeking information that fits with preexisting ideas or beliefs. With the rise of media outlets that are thought to have ideological or partisan slant, many people have expressed concern that citizens will no longer expose themselves to ideas that contradict their own. Of course, there are now plenty of partisan and ideological websites that people could also use to gather information that fits with their predispositions. If selective exposure does happen, then it seems likely that information provided by the media and political campaigns would have little effect on potential voters. Indeed, how could the news media or campaigns persuade people if they only seek information that matches their preexisting ideas? The idea that information from the media and political campaigns likely has only minor effects on individuals (because they ignore contradictory information and seek out information that they already agree with) is called the "minimal effects thesis."

The idea of selective exposure has been a hot topic recently, as politics has become more and more polarized. Interestingly, the evidence on selective exposure has been fairly mixed. Some studies have reported evidence that partisan attachments are strongly correlated with self-reported media consumption habits.[26] But there may be errors in self-reports on media consumption. Political scientist Brendan Nyhan has pointed out that "liberals or conservatives may be prone to exaggerating their exposure to ideologically consistent news outlets."[27] In short, during public opinion surveys people may feel pressure to say that they use media sources that they think match with their ideology or partisanship. Nyhan goes on to note that "it turns out that the media people are actually exposed to both online and offline is much more diverse and heterogeneous than people's self-reports suggest."[28] Indeed, a number of academic studies have found that most people actually get information from fairly centrist media outlets and that only a small percentage of people get all of their information from ideologically similar media sources. One thing to keep in mind when considering the impact of partisan or ideological attachments on media consumption is that media consumption may not be the cause of different interpretations of political events and issues. As Brendan Nyhan nicely points out, "Democrats and Republicans don't see the world so differently because they see different news; rather, they see the news differently because they're Democrats and Republicans in the first place."[29]

It has been challenging to study the effect that the media has on people due to the issues raised above. One interesting study worth mentioning (by political scientists Alan Gerber, Dean Kaplan, and Daniel Bergan) used an experiment to determine whether exposure to a liberal or conservative newspaper influences people's attitudes and behaviors. In the study, the researchers sent subjects complimentary subscriptions of either *The Washington Post*, a liberal newspaper, or *The Washington Times*, a conservative newspaper, for one month. The subjects were randomly assigned to receive one of the papers or to be in a control group comprised of people who did not receive either one. The researchers found that those who received the *Post* were more likely to vote for the Democratic gubernatorial candidate in the state where the experiment was conducted. It appears that exposure to ideological news coverage can have an impact on political behavior, although the question of how long such effects persist is an open one.

One additional concern that many people express, especially when elections are occurring, is that the political advertisements created by candidates and run by media outlets have become too negative. The argument against negative advertisements usually begins with the idea that many people do not like the mudslinging, criticism, or attacks that often appear in modern political advertisements. It has become quite clear that negativity is now commonplace in American politics and campaign messages, associated with the growing partisan polarization. One widely held idea about this negativity is that it repels people from elections and politics in general, leading to decreased voter turnout. Again, it is interesting to ask what political scientists have discovered regarding the impact of negative campaign messages on voters. A few years ago, a group of political scientists conducted an analysis of all of the studies on negative advertising that they could identify (nearly 60 separate studies). Their synthesis of previous studies found that *"the research literature provides no general support for the hypothesis that negative political campaigning depresses voter turnout. If anything, negative campaigning more frequently appears to have a slight mobilizing effect."*[30] Often, even negative advertisements provide valuable information to the electorate. Indeed, many negative ads provide contrasting information about political candidates. Because ordinary Americans pay little attention to politics, the information provided by campaign ads, even if it is negatively oriented, can be helpful. It turns out that most ads sponsored by candidates are positive in tone, while parties and interest groups are more inclined to sponsor the negative attack ads.[31] Research has also suggested that negative ads are "more likely to focus on issues, are more specific and contain many more facts than positive ads."[32]

Negativity in politics is different from incivility in politics. Uncivil attacks go "beyond facts and differences, and move instead towards name-calling, contempt, and derision of the opponent."[33] Although many people have suggested that incivility in campaign ads is damaging to democracy, one recent study indicates that "the public will not melt in response to harsh exchanges—even those that are uncivil—and might even modestly profit from them in some cases. This should be good news to those who observe and study politics because it suggests that the American electorate is quite resilient to the nasty exchanges now prevalent in U.S. political discourse."[34] Thus, it seems that concerns about negativity and incivility in political advertisements may be overstated. Rather than having damaging effects on the electorate, negativity and incivility in campaign messages appear to have some positive effects, especially when it comes to increasing voter turnout and political interest.[35]

Recent changes in the regulatory landscape may mitigate the potentially harmful consequences of negative campaign ads. For instance, it is often difficult for voters to understand whether a candidate created a campaign ad or whether an outside group created it. As of 2014, the Federal Communications Commission has required every broadcast television station in the country to post copies of contracts and other information about the political advertisements they are airing. The idea here is to give voters access to documents detailing who is buying campaign commercials and how much money is being spent.[36] In addition, there are also disclosure laws for federal campaign ads in which those who have paid for or sponsored the ad must identify themselves. Of course, increasing access to information about who purchases campaign ads and requiring sponsors to identify themselves in political ads will not solve all of the problems that people have with campaigning in U.S. elections, but making the process more transparent seems like an important way to enhance the ability of the public to become better informed and to hold people accountable. Even so, it seems likely that additional innovations will be necessary in order to alter people's pessimistic perceptions of political campaigns.

Ways to Improve the Media

As we did in the previous chapters, we would like to end by providing some ideas on how media coverage in the United States could be improved.

- We noted above that partisan/ideological biases in the media may not be as strong as people suspect, though there are certainly outlets that are consistently liberal or conservative. If people are concerned about getting one-sided information from media outlets, they could intentionally consult a variety of sources that cover politics. Why not watch a variety of programs or visit a number of different websites (to cross-check information) about political issues of interest? There are now media outlets that cover politics from the left, right, middle, and a range of different ideological perspectives.
- Citizens may find it difficult to know what political information is accurate. There are now numerous fact-checking websites that analyze claims reported in the news and made by politicians. Few people may know about such websites, but they do exist and could be helpful as people try to learn about the news. The three big fact-checking websites include PolitiFact, FactCheck.org, and The Fact Checker of *The Washington Post*. These three websites publish about 75% of the fact checks.[37]
- Local newspapers and broadcasts could devote more coverage to politics. Studies have indicated that political news from these outlets can be quite influential. If citizens are not satisfied with local news coverage, they could consider contacting media outlets with suggestions on how to improve their coverage of politics.
- Rather than relying on the mass media to learn about politics, citizens could obtain information of interest directly from the government or from other organizations that track government activities. There are websites that track campaign finance, congressional voting on a range of issues, lobbying activities, and many more political activities. There is now more transparency in government than ever before and citizens could start learning about politics by gathering their own information.

Notes

1. Dahl, Robert. 1983. *Dilemmas of Pluralist Democracy.* New Haven, CT: Yale.
2. http://www.stateofthemedia.org/2011/newspapers-essay/data-page-6/.
3. http://www.princeton.edu/wwseconpapers/papers/wwsdp236.pdf.

4. http://www.princeton.edu/wwseconpapers/papers/wwsdp236.pdf.

5. http://media-cmi.com/downloads/CMI_Discussion_Paper_Circulation_Trends_102813.pdf.

6. http://www.pewinternet.org/files/old-media/Files/Reports/2011/Pew%20Knight%20Local%20News%20Report%20FINAL.pdf.

7. Ibid.

8. http://www.pewinternet.org/data-trend/social-media/social-media-use-by-age-group/.

9. http://www.pewinternet.org/2012/09/04/politics-on-social-networking-sites/.

10. http://www.pewinternet.org/2014/11/03/cell-phones-social-media-and-campaign-2014/.

11. McCombs, M.E., and D.L. Shaw. 1972. "The Agenda-Setting Function of Mass Media." *Public Opinion Quarterly* 36 (Summer): 176–187.

12. Cohen, Bernard. 1963. *The Press and Foreign Policy.* Princeton, NJ: Princeton University Press.

13. http://politicalticker.blogs.cnn.com/2013/09/27/poll-obamacare-vs-affordable-care-act/.

14. Druckman, James. 2005. "Media Matter: How Newspapers and Television News Cover Campaigns and Influence Voters." *Political Communication* 22: 463–481.

15. Panagopoulos, Costas, ed. 2007. *Rewiring Politics: Presidential Nominating Conventions in the Media Age.* Baton Rouge, LA: Louisiana State University Press.

16. Green, Donald, and Alan Gerber. 2008. *Get Out the Vote: How to Increase Voter Turnout, 2nd Edition.* Washington, DC: Brookings.

17. Gerber, Alan S., Dean Karlan, and Daniel Bergan. 2009. "Does the Media Matter? A Field Experiment Measuring the Effect of Newspapers on Voting Behavior and Political Opinions." *American Economic Journal: Applied Economics* 1: 35–52.

18. http://www.people-press.org/2011/09/22/press-widely-criticized-but-trusted-more-than-other-institutions/.

19. D'Alessio, Dave. 2012. *Media Bias in Presidential Election Coverage, 1948–2008.* Lanham, MD: Lexington Books.

20. http://onlinelibrary.wiley.com/doi/10.1111/j.1460-2466.2000.tb02866.x/abstract.

21. http://www.pewresearch.org/fact-tank/2013/06/05/is-msnbc-the-place-for-opinion/.

22. http://www.people-press.org/2011/09/22/press-widely-criticized-but-trusted-more-than-other-institutions/.

23. http://www.niemanlab.org/2012/06/how-do-you-tell-when-the-news-is-biased/.

24. Schaffner, Brian. 2006. "Local News Coverage and the Incumbency Advantage in the U.S. House." *Legislative Studies Quarterly* 31: 491–511.

25. Ibid.

26. http://www.journalism.org/files/2014/10/Political-Polarization-and-Media-Habits-FINAL-REPORT.pdf.

27. http://www.nytimes.com/2014/10/25/upshot/americans-dont-live-in-information-cocoons.html?_r=0&abt=0002&abg=1.

28. Ibid.

29. Ibid.

30. Lau, Richard, Lee Sigelman, and Ivy Brown Rovner. 2007. "The Effects of Negative Political Campaigns: A Meta-Analytic Reassessment." *Journal of Politics* 69: 1176–1209.

31. Franz, Michael, Paul B. Freedman, Kenneth M. Goldstein, and Travis N. Ridout. 2007. *Campaign Advertising and American Democracy.* Philadelphia, PA: Temple University Press.
32. http://articles.latimes.com/2008/mar/17/opinion/oe-geer17.
33. Brooks, Deborah, and John Geer. 2007. "Beyond Negativity: The Effects of Incivility on the Electorate." *American Journal of Political Science* 51: 1–16.
34. Ibid.
35. Ibid.
36. http://sunlightfoundation.com/blog/2014/06/30/new-fcc-online-political-ad-disclosure-rule-exposes-dark-money-tv-buys/.
37. Marietta, Morgan. 2014. "Your Facts or Mine? The Political Epistemology of the Online Fact Check Industry." Paper presented at the 12th Annual Pre Conference on Political Communication.

9

VOTE CHOICE

Elections are the key mechanism that enables citizens to hold elected officials responsible for their actions in office. Given the importance of vote choices, it is natural to ask how citizens make them on Election Day. Why do they vote for one candidate over another? This is one of the most interesting and commonly asked questions during any election cycle. In an ideal world, the decision-making process would look something like this: Citizens would be aware of the different policies and programs that candidates have stated they will pursue if elected, they would spend time learning about the candidates and their appropriateness for office, and they would use that knowledge to choose among the candidates—presumably selecting the candidate who best represented their preferences. Do ordinary Americans typically engage in these kinds of processes before making electoral choices? Do they conduct thorough investigations and acquire detailed information before deciding how to vote? Do they know about the policies that elected officials have implemented or pledged to implement in the future?

In this chapter, we discuss the most important factors that influence voter choice. We focus on the impact of cues and shortcuts, partisanship, ideology, candidate traits, political issues, and social group memberships or identities. We also discuss the ways in which political campaigns can influence vote choice. In general, most citizens are not well-informed about politics and do not invest heavily in acquiring detailed candidate and policy information. We point out that voters often make political choices "on the cheap" by using information cues and voting shortcuts. The problem is not that detailed information is unavailable, but rather that it is often too costly (or "irrational") for voters to seek out or acquire such information. Although the use of voting shortcuts and cues may be convenient, technology has made it much easier for voters to gain detailed information about candidates and policies during elections. If voters invest more time in learning about political candidates, they may be able to make more informed electoral choices and be able to hold elected officials more accountable.

Political Knowledge in the American Electorate

For years now, political scientists have noted the lack of knowledge that ordinary Americans have about politics. Indeed, a well-known book by Michael Delli Carpini and Scott Keeter, *What Americans Know about Politics and Why It Matters* (published in 1996), documented that a large slice of the electorate knows very little about politics. The good news is that people who are well-informed tend to participate at high rates; the bad news is that there are biases in terms of who is well-informed— individuals who are disadvantaged socially and economically are the least knowledgeable about politics. Study after study has confirmed that the American public has little political knowledge. When asked basic questions about the structure of government and current political leaders, Americans typically perform quite poorly. A recent survey asked native-born Americans to take a quiz containing ten questions from the U.S. citizenship and immigration civics exam. The results of the survey were quite interesting: 85% could not define "the rule of law," 75% did not know the function of the judicial branch, 71% were unable to identify the Constitution as the "supreme law of the land," 63% could not name one of their state senators, 62% did not know the name of the Speaker of the U.S. House of Representatives, 62% could not identify the governor of their state, and 57% could not define an "amendment."[1] A 2011 poll conducted by Pew Research showed that just 38% of people knew which party had the majority in the U.S. House, 43% knew who the Speaker of the House was at the time, and 57% knew the current unemployment rate (within a few percent).[2] When it comes to understanding the details of things like how the government spends money, knowledge levels also tend to be quite low. A recent poll by Pew Research asked a representative sample the following question: "On which of the following activities does the U.S. government currently spend the most money...foreign aid, interest on the debt, social security, or transportation?" In answering the question, 33% of people said foreign aid. Of those four choices, the U.S. government spends the most on Social Security (only 20% of people knew this) and the least on foreign aid.[3] The U.S. government actually spends less than 1% of its budget on foreign aid and yet many people believe that this is where most of the federal budget is spent. As a final example, a 2014 survey asked a sample of Americans what the current unemployment rate was in the United States. The correct answer was 6% but the average guess was 32%.[4]

The details about specific public policies are also cloudy for many ordinary Americans. A recent example illuminates the lack of knowledge that people have about public policies. One of the most important pieces of legislation that has been passed in the past few decades is the Affordable Care Act (ACA) of 2010. The ACA has captured a great deal of media attention and has been a salient issue for quite some time now. One poll asked a sample of Americans whether different provisions were included in the ACA. For many of the provisions, large portions of Americans provided incorrect answers about what was included or not. For example, 60% of people gave incorrect answers about medical loss ratios (the ratio that must be spent on healthcare versus overhead), 54% gave incorrect answers about closing the Medicare gaps, 48% gave incorrect answers about tax credits to small businesses to buy insurance, 47% gave incorrect answers about guaranteed issue, 46% gave incorrect answers about increasing the Medicare payroll tax, 42% gave incorrect answers about health insurance exchanges, and 41% gave incorrect answers about Medicaid expansion.[5] It is interesting to note that despite the lack of knowledge on some of the key provisions in the ACA, public opinion about the ACA is quite polarized by partisanship. According to a recent poll asking about approval of the ACA, 68% of Republicans view the law unfavorably, while a majority of Democrats (58%) view it favorably.[6] Despite the lack of knowledge that exists about the ACA, many people have strong opinions. Given the figures provided above and the fact that the ACA is about 1,000 pages long, it seems unlikely that many people are familiar with the major ideas within the act (and very few people have probably read the act).

So where are people getting their opinions about the ACA? The answer is fairly straightforward: from cues provided by political elites. Political scientists have long known that average citizens take cues from politicians and party leaders. In short, citizens look to political elites to see what they are saying about different policies and programs. Rather than reading a policy, which seems quite burdensome and time consuming, many citizens turn to people they perceive as being experts. Since many Republicans in Congress have objected to the ACA, it makes sense that many Republican identifiers would adopt that position as well. Since many Democrats in Congress and President Obama have praised the ACA, it makes sense that many Democratic identifiers would approve of the legislation. This kind of thing happens on all kinds of different policy issues.

Partisanship

Given the importance of party cues in the above example, it is probably not surprising to find out that an individual's party identification—the psychological connection many citizens have with a political party—is the most powerful predictor of how they will vote on Election Day. The idea that people have psychological connections to parties and use those attachments when making their choices emerged in the 1950s by a group of political scientists and psychologists at the University of Michigan (an approach that became known as the "Michigan model"). In fact, scholars believe partisanship is linked closely to citizens' social identity. Individual political partisanship exerts a significant effect on voter choice, and the power of partisanship is readily observable in recent elections. In the 2012 election, for example, 92% of Democrats voted for Barack Obama, while 93% of Republicans voted for Mitt Romney.[7] By matching a person's partisanship, an individual predisposition, with the partisanship of a candidate, it becomes fairly easy to make a choice. Candidate party affiliations are a very important and convenient cue that people can use when voting.

One thing worth noting is that not everyone in the electorate develops an attachment to a specific party; some voters are independents. Although media commentary might lead one to believe that independent voters are the largest group in the electorate, it turns out that most independents are actually "closet partisans." In other words, most people who initially say that they are politically independent will admit that they actually lean toward one party or the other when asked a second time if they prefer one party over the other. And most of these independent "leaners" behave just like strong partisans—they vote for the party they lean toward at very high rates. In the end, only a small slice of the electorate is truly independent (about 10% in recent years).[8] Although independents are often seen as the group that is "up for grabs" during any election, it is important to be mindful of the fact that independents tend to be less politically engaged and less interested in politics than partisans. Thus, it can be hard for campaigns to influence independents.

Information Cues

Candidates' party attachments are not the only cues that are available on ballots. Incumbency is also a valuable cue that voters often rely on when making choices. In the United States, incumbency is a powerful shortcut when voters are looking at a ballot, and voters reelect incumbents at remarkably high rates (upwards of 90% in most congressional elections). Political scientists have also demonstrated that the order in which candidate names appear on the ballot can influence voters. One recent study, for example, found that candidates whose names appear first on the ballot do about 2% better than the following candidates (that's certainly enough to change the outcome of a close election).[9] When voters lack substantive information or if they are ambivalent about candidates, peripheral cues like ballot order can be used to help make choices. Political scientist Jon Krosnick has pointed out that "voters apparently feel an obligation or desire to vote even when they have no basis for choosing a candidate and are drawn to the first name they read."[10] Things like incumbency, partisanship, and candidate name order can simplify the voting process, making it easier for voters to make choices among a set of candidates.

Political scientists have long argued that voters use cues and shortcuts to help ease decision making, a process that can lead to "low-information rationality."[11] In short, by relying on cues from elites or by using information shortcuts, voters can make choices as if they were more informed. It is hard to see how candidate name order would be a useful tool, but partisanship and incumbency could certainly provide some information to voters. Although some may not like the use of these tools to make vote choices, decades of research have indicated that many voters use these things on Election Day. Below, we discuss some of the problems that can occur when voters rely on cues and shortcuts.

Ideology

One factor that also elicits some attention during elections is the role of ideology. In public opinion surveys, voter ideology is typically conceptualized along a continuum ranging from liberal to conservative (for an excellent and detailed account of American ideology check out Morgan Marietta's book, *A Citizen's Guide to American Ideology: Conservatism and Liberalism in Contemporary Politics,* which is part of this series). Just to be clear, partisanship and ideology do not refer to the same concept. Many people have come to see these things as synonyms. Although it is certainly true that partisanship and ideology have become more strongly correlated over time in the United States, partisanship and ideology are distinct concepts. A partisan attachment refers to a cognitive or emotional connection to a political party. An ideology refers to "a vision of the ideal society, along with the means of achieving it."[12] When considering the impact of voter ideology during elections, it is important to point out that studies in political science have demonstrated that most voters lack a consistent outlook about issues and public policies. In short, most people do not have strong underlying ideologies that guide their opinions (there are clearly passionate ideologues, but they are a small minority), though citizens typically do have other belief structures like values. Indeed, political scientists have long known that the public often holds "non-attitudes," that is, opinions that are random over time or internally inconsistent, and that many people form opinions about issues on the basis of "top-of-the-head" considerations.[13] In other words, many people will choose to support or oppose a policy depending on the mix of considerations sampled from the top of their head—with factors that are salient in a person's mind at that time being more likely to be used than factors that are not salient.

Ideological labels, like party attachments, have a great deal of emotional value. Even though few ordinary Americans have coherent ideologies, the terms "liberal" and "conservative" appear to help voters figure out who is on their "team" and who is on the opposing side. This is consistent with the ideas outlined above regarding the value and utility of political partisanship. Ideological allegiances often play an important role during U.S. elections. Indeed, in the 2012 presidential election, 86% of self-identified liberals voted for Obama and 82% of self-identified conservatives voted for Romney.[14] It is worth pointing out that political elites—those who are heavily involved in or knowledgeable about politics—do tend to have strong belief systems.[15] They tend to see the connections that exist across issues, exhibit attitude stability over time, and have a consistent outlook on politics and public policy. In short, they think in ideological terms. These kinds of people, however, represent a very thin slice of the American electorate.

Recent scholarship presents an interesting view on the origins of individual political ideology. Political scientists John Hibbing, Kevin Smith, and John Alford, among others, have argued that human biology—in other words, our genes—predisposes us to see the world in different ways.[16] According to this view, whether our outlook on the world of politics is liberal or conservative may have as much to do with our genetics as it does with our surroundings; researchers have also linked partisanship and even voting to specific genes. Rather than being determinative, however (genes do not dictate what we think or how we behave in politics), biology may predispose us to thinking and behaving in certain ways. While these studies are perhaps too few and new to be conclusive, they hint at intriguing possibilities about how we can understand the nature and origins of ideological tendencies.

Political Issues

One thing that many people say when they learn about the effects that partisanship, ideology, incumbency, and candidate name order have in U.S. elections is that perhaps some people are not fully investigating the candidates they are selecting. Do people really know what the incumbent candidate has done while in office? Do they know which policies the incumbent has voted for or against? Do people really know why they like the liberal candidate more than the conservative one? Does the fact that a candidate is listed first on the ballot tell a voter anything about the candidate's qualifications for office? As the figures presented above illustrate, the American public often has minimal knowledge of politics. Most people do not research the votes that members of Congress have cast. Most people do not spend time attending candidate debates or forums. And most people do not gather information about each candidate's policy positions. When it comes to elections, the role of political issues often attracts a great deal of media attention. The media often create the impression that issues are central to voter decision making. But do people really vote on the basis of political issues? People who are political junkies often have very strong attitudes and preferences about policies and issues. They know where they stand and they know where different parties and candidates stand. Of course, very few people are political junkies. It sometimes surprises people to find out that the American public generally does not place a lot of weight on political issues when deciding on political candidates. Most Americans are simply not interested enough or motivated to go and learn about the details of different policies. It is important to note that many people will simply express support for the policies that they know the politicians they support have endorsed. There are some issue voters out there, but they only represent a small portion of the electorate.

Although few people are issue voters, there are certainly some assessments that many people use when making electoral choices. The state of the economy, for example, has long been one of the most important considerations for voters in elections. In his classic book on elections, *Retrospective Voting in American National Elections,* political scientist Morris Fiorina noted that when the economy is doing well, voters tend to reward the incumbent party and when the economy is doing poorly, voters tend to punish that party.[17] We should note, though, that the relationship between the state of the economy matters much more in presidential elections than in congressional midterm elections.[18] The idea that voters reflect back on factors like the state of the economy (or other

144

conditions) and use their assessments to guide electoral decision making is known as "retrospective voting." The basic ideas of retrospective voting were originally outlined by economist Anthony Downs in *An Economic Theory of Democracy*, which was published in 1957. One of Downs's core ideas was that voters think in terms of expected utilities. Basically, voters will compare the utility (positive benefits or feelings) they got out of the incumbent party to the utility that the other party might have provided. Voters then cast their ballots for the party that maximizes their expected utility. If the expected utility of voting for the incumbent party is less than the expected utility of voting for the nonincumbent party, then the voter should not vote for the incumbent party. There are, of course, some obvious limitations to this idea. What if voters are not well-informed about politics? What if voters are myopic or misattribute responsibility for good or bad conditions? What if voters make assessments about political issues or conditions through partisan or ideological lenses?

When it comes to evaluations of the economy, it is clear that most voters are not conducting detailed research about economic policies or conditions. People have a basic sense of whether things are good or bad and they use that sense to make a choice. Although this seems like a reasonable approach, we should point out that there are some limitations to this method. One thing that is worth mentioning about economic assessments is that partisanship and ideology often work to shape how people view economic events and performance. In other words, partisan and ideological attachments serve as lenses through which people view the political world. It is interesting to note that studies in political science have shown that Democrats and Republicans view objective economic conditions in very different ways. For instance, when a Democratic president is in office, Democratic identifiers tend to hold positive assessments of the economy (even if objective indicators show that it is not performing particularly well) and Republican identifiers tend to hold negative assessments of the economy (even if objective indicators show that it is performing well). The same is true in reverse: When a Republican president is in office, Republican identifiers tend to hold positive assessments of the economy regardless of objective facts, and Democratic identifiers tend to hold negative assessments.[19] It is also interesting to note that voters tend to give more weight to recent economic conditions during elections, especially economic conditions that occur immediately before an election.[20] Thus, although a president may have served for four years, voters may really only consider the economic conditions in the year before the election. It is also important to point out that studies have demonstrated that irrelevant events can impact assessments of incumbents and incumbent performance. As we noted above, one idea about political accountability suggests that incumbents should be rewarded when people believe that incumbents have implemented good policies and improved economic conditions. Of course, there are limits on what incumbents can and cannot control or impact. Presumably, voters shouldn't reward or punish incumbents for things that they have no control over. Interestingly, a number of political science studies have shown that voters reward incumbent candidates for things like sports team wins and punish incumbents for things like shark attacks, which have nothing to do with incumbent performance in government.[21] It is also interesting to note that presidents have little control over the national economy, though they take the credit or blame regardless. The same could also be said for governors and mayors when it comes to state and local economies.

Candidate Traits

Another factor that people often wonder about during elections are candidate traits—things like personality attributes and physical appearance. During presidential elections, the media have come to love talking about the "beer test." In short, they enjoy asking the question *Which candidate would you rather sit down and have a beer with?* This question is usually discussed in the context of voter perceptions of how relatable and likeable the candidates are. Of course, there are many other attributes that draw attention—candidate attractiveness, whether candidates seem honest, whether candidates come from political families, how much personal wealth candidates have, whether candidates seem intelligent, and the list goes on and on. Given the media's attention to candidate traits, one might suspect that voter perceptions about candidate traits have important effects during elections. During the 2012 presidential election, candidate traits received quite a bit of attention. Many news stories covered Obama's likeability, Romney's looks, Obama's educational background, and Romney's wealth. In general, political scientists have not found strong evidence that voter assessments of candidate traits matter a great deal in elections, especially in elections for high-level offices like the presidency where there tends to be a great deal of information available to voters. Political scientist Morris Fiorina has noted, "Other things being equal, it is no doubt better for a candidate to be liked than disliked, but when other things are not equal, historical data suggest that a candidate's likability is a relatively minor factor in deciding modern presidential elections."[22] He goes on to point out that "in the 13 elections between 1952 and 2000, Republican candidates won four of the six in which they had higher personal ratings than the Democrats, while Democratic candidates lost four of the seven elections in which they had higher ratings than the Republicans. Not much evidence of a big likability effect here."[23] Partisanship and ideology often play a role in shaping voter perceptions of the candidates. Republican voters tend to give Republican candidates more favorable assessments than they give Democrats and Democratic voters tend to give Democratic candidates more favorable assessments than they give Republicans.[24]

Social Groups

Social group memberships and identities also shape vote choice. The investigation of the influence of social factors on electoral choices has been traced to *The People's Choice,* a book published in 1944. One of the most interesting ideas presented in that book is that the social groups to which people belong play a decisive role in their vote choices. In addition to partisanship, political scientists have long been interested in the effects of attributes like race, ethnicity, religious affiliation, and union membership on the vote. In general, social identities or memberships, if they are politically relevant (or if they can be made politically relevant), can play an important role in shaping the way that people vote. In the United States, race has typically been an important factor. Since the civil rights era, for example, African Americans have voted for Democratic candidates at very high rates. In 2008, 95% of African Americans voted for the Democratic presidential candidate and in 2012 the figure was 93%. Union membership represents another group identity that plays a role in voter decision making. Union members tend to favor Democrats in U.S. elections. During the 2012 presidential election, for example, 58% of voters who lived in a household that had at least one union member voted for the Democratic candidate. Although not every social group identity or membership has this pronounced an effect on the vote, social attachments can certainly play a powerful role in voter decision making (even after accounting for factors like partisanship and ideology). Table 9.1 provides a look at how different groups voted in the 2012 presidential election. Although not all of the groups show large differences in vote choice, there are pronounced differences for some of the groups. Because of the deficits in political information we noted above, social group identities and attachments can provide a way of simplifying the voting process by helping people connect their interests to parties and candidates.

Table 9.1 Vote Choice by Social Groups (2012 Presidential Election)

Group	Percent Voting for Obama (Democrat)	Percent Voting for Romney (Republican)
Men	45%	52%
Women	55%	44%
White	39%	59%
African American	93%	6%
Latino	71%	27%
Asian	73%	26%
Democrat	92%	7%
Republican	6%	93%
Independent	45%	50%
18–29 Years Old	60%	37%
30–44 Years Old	52%	45%
45–64 Years Old	47%	51%
65 and Older	44%	56%
Liberal	86%	11%
Moderate	56%	41%
Conservative	17%	82%
Income less than $50,000 per year	60%	38%
$50,000–$100,000 per year	46%	52%
$100,000 or more per year	44%	54%
Anyone in household a union member (Yes)	58%	40%
Anyone in household a union member (No)	49%	48%
Protestant	42%	57%
Catholic	50%	48%
Other	74%	23%
None	70%	26%
Attend religious services weekly	39%	59%
Attend religious services occasionally	55%	43%
Never attend religious services	62%	34%

Note: Data from 2012 CNN Exit Poll webpage, http://www.cnn.com/election/2012/results/race/president.

Political Campaigns and Vote Choice

One remaining factor that we have not discussed is the role of political campaigns in voter decision making. Given the vast amounts of money that are spent by campaigns, it is interesting to consider whether these efforts influence the vote choices that citizens make on Election Day. Scholars have identified a number of potential ways that political campaigns can impact voters. One thing that campaigns do is to provide voters with information—they can help voters learn. We noted above that most Americans are not particularly well-informed about politics. Exposure to campaign information via commercials, news articles, radio advertisements, campaign mailers, and television coverage can provide potential voters with a great deal of information about who the candidates are and what they represent. As political scientist Sunshine Hillygus has pointed out, "Campaign learning helps to decrease the incumbency advantage and increase issue voting."[25]

A second way that campaigns can influence vote choice is through "priming," or influencing voters to consider a specific issue that they otherwise may not have. Campaigns can draw attention to certain issues and downplay others, which might influence their level of importance in voters' minds. It makes sense that if a candidate was advantaged by economic conditions, the candidate would want to play up that issue during the campaign to get voters to connect those economic conditions to their vote choices on Election Day.[26] There is some evidence that the failure to connect positive economic conditions to their candidate can be quite costly for the campaign.[27] Campaigns can also serve to increase the connection between voters' preexisting attributes (partisanship, social group memberships, ideology, etc.) and their vote choice.[28] In other words, campaigns can help remind voters of how their predispositions should be connected to their vote.

A third way that campaigns can influence vote choice is through persuasion. Given the importance of partisan and ideological attachments, persuasion can be quite difficult for campaigns, although it is certainly possible. Political science research has shown that some political events and activities, like presidential conventions and television advertisements, are capable of persuading some voters to change their vote choices. Large-scale political events that occur at points during the campaign process when voters are still looking for information about the candidates can be particularly influential. For instance, the presidential nominating conventions, which typically occur when information about the candidates is relatively limited (a few months before the November elections), have been shown to generate bumps in candidate support that persist into Election Day.[29] Research at the individual level has also illustrated that campaigns can have a persuasive effect on voters. For example, one study on the 2000 presidential election found that "mismatched partisans, undecided voters, and Independents were particularly likely to change their vote preferences following the campaign events [debates and conventions], offering strong evidence of both partisan activation and persuasion effects."[30] In close elections, getting a small slice of the electorate to change their vote choice could be very important.

Overall, the discussion above implies campaigns can affect election outcomes, even if they do not always exert very strong effects. As we discuss above, election outcomes are often predictable from "fundamental" factors, like the economy and presidential approval, that are generally in place long before the campaigns unfold (or even before the candidates are selected). Most voters, guided by partisan or other predispositions, usually decide how they will vote in national elections long before the campaign ends (many decide before it even starts). Studies of pre-election polls reveal voter preferences change modestly over the course of an election; nevertheless, there is evidence of meaningful change, often attributed to campaign events or other developments, and this can be consequential, especially in close races.

Ways to Improve Voter Decision Making

As we did in the previous chapters, we would like to end by providing some ideas on how voter decision making in the United States could be improved.

- People regularly complain about not being able to find good information about politicians and political issues. There are now dozens of websites that provide political analysis. There are websites that track legislators' voting patterns, rate legislators on different issues, track the productivity of legislators, and fact-check statements made by politicians and media outlets. If citizens want to become more informed about the political process and have more information when making voting decisions, they could use the wealth of information that is at their disposal.

- It is often difficult for citizens to keep up with local politics because it usually does not attract as much attention as national politics. To increase public understanding of local government and politics, cities or nonprofits could work to develop websites that provide an analysis of important local issues. Of course, it would be important to make citizens aware that such information is available. Studies have shown that local news coverage is an important way that people learn about local politics. Thus, it may be important for citizens to pressure local media outlets to devote more attention to local political issues.

- It may be possible to change electoral ballots to make it easier for voters to make informed choices. Many local elections are nonpartisan and do not include information about candidate party attachments. The lack of this information cue can make it harder for voters to make decisions (if partisanship tells voters something about what a candidate might do in office, it could be a useful cue). States or localities could consider allowing candidates to provide more information than just their names on the ballot. The presence of cues can be very helpful for voters, especially in low-information contexts.

- Citizens could pressure state and local elected officials (or other groups interested in civic engagement) to develop civic education policies that target the costs voters might incur when acquiring political information. The costs of becoming informed about politics (e.g., buying a newspaper subscription, having Internet access, etc.) can be high for some members of society. States or localities could develop policies that make it easier for voters to obtain political information. Such policies could include things like voter guides, mailings, civic education programs, websites, or a combination of these things.

- Cities could consider altering their electoral process to improve voter decision making. The city of San Francisco, for example, uses something called ranked choice voting (RCV), which allows voters to rank up to three candidates, in order of preference, when voting. The system works in a very straightforward way. If a candidate receives a majority (50%+1) of the first-choice votes cast for that office, he or she is elected to office. If a candidate does not receive a majority of the first-choice votes cast, the election moves on to an elimination process. The candidate with the fewest first-choice votes gets eliminated. Each vote cast for that candidate will be transferred to the voter's next preferred choice among the remaining candidates. The process continues until one candidate receives a majority of the vote and then that person is elected to office.[31] This system could offer a number of benefits to voters. For example, this process gives voters a chance to rank as many or as few candidates as they would like—without having to worry that ranking less preferred candidates harms the chances of their top candidate.[32]

Notes

1. http://www.usnews.com/news/blogs/washington-whispers/2012/04/30/study-one-in-three-americans-fails-naturalization-civics-test.
2. http://www.people-press.org/2011/03/31/well-known-clinton-and-gadhafi-little-known-who-controls-congress/.
3. http://www.washingtonpost.com/blogs/wonkblog/wp/2014/10/02/americans-have-no-idea-how-the-government-spends-money/.

4. http://kottke.org/14/11/the-united-states-of-ignorance.
5. http://kff.org/health-reform/poll-finding/march-2013-tracking-poll/.
6. http://kff.org/health-reform/slide/trends-in-partisan-views-of-the-aca/.
7. http://www.cnn.com/election/2012/results/race/president.
8. Keith, Bruce, David Magelby, Candice Nelson, Elizabeth Orr, Mark Westlye, and Raymond Wolfinger. 1992. *The Myth of the Independent Voter*. Berkeley, CA: University of California Press.
9. Chen, Eric, Gabor Simonovits, Jon Krosnick, and Josh Pasek. Forthcoming. 2014. "The Impact of Candidate Name Order on Election Outcomes in North Dakota." *Electoral Studies*.
10. http://www.nytimes.com/2006/11/04/opinion/04krosnick.html.
11. Popkin, Samuel. 1994. *The Reasoning Voter: Communication and Persuasion in Presidential Campaigns*, 2nd edition. Chicago, IL: University of Chicago Press.
12. Jacoby, Bill. 2009. "Ideology and Vote Choice in the 2004 Election." *Electoral Studies* 28: 584–594.
13. Converse, Philip. 1964. "The Nature of Belief Systems in Mass Publics." In D.E. Apter (Ed.), *Ideology and Discontent*. New York, NY: Free Press. Zaller, John. 1992. *The Nature and Origin of Mass Opinion*. Cambridge, UK: Cambridge University Press.
14. http://www.cnn.com/election/2012/results/race/president.
15. Converse, Philip. 1964. "The Nature of Belief Systems in Mass Publics." In D.E. Apter (Ed.), *Ideology and Discontent*. New York, NY: Free Press.
16. Hibbing, John, Kevin Smith, and John Alford. 2014. *Predisposed: Liberals, Conservatives, and the Biology of Political Differences*. New York, NY: Routledge. Fowler, James, and Christopher Dawes. 2013. "In Defense of Genopolitics." *American Political Science Review* 107: 362–374.
17. Fiorina, Morris. 1981. *Retrospective Voting in American National Elections*. New Haven, CT: Yale.
18. http://www.nytimes.com/2014/11/04/upshot/the-economy-and-voters-perception-of-it-are-two-very-different-things.html?_r=1&abt=0002&abg=1.
19. Bartels, Larry. 2002. "Beyond the Running Tally: Partisan Bias in Political Perceptions." *Political Behavior* 24: 117–150.
20. Sides, John, and Lynn Vavreck. 2012. *The Gamble: Choice and Chance in the 2012 Presidential Election*. Princeton, NJ: Princeton University Press.
21. Healy, Andrew, Neil Malhotra, and Cecilia Jyunjunk Mo. 2010. "Irrelevant Events Affect Voters' Evaluations of Government Performance." *Proceedings of the National Academy of Sciences of the United States* 107: 12804–12809. Achen, Christopher, and Larry Bartels. 2013. "Blind Retrospection: Why Shark Attacks Are Bad for Democracy." *Vanderbilt Center for the Study of Democratic Institutions* Working Paper 5–2013.
22. http://campaignstops.blogs.nytimes.com/2012/06/07/youre-likable-enough-mitt/.
23. Ibid.
24. Hayes, Danny. 2005. "Candidate Qualities through a Partisan Lens: A Theory of Trait Ownership." *American Journal of Political Science* 49: 908–923.
25. Hillygus, D. Sunshine. 2010. "Campaign Effects on Vote Choice." In Leighley, J. (Ed) *The Oxford Handbook of American Elections and Political Behavior*, 327–345.
26. Vavreck, Lynn. 2009. *The Message Matters: The Economy and Presidential Campaigns*. Princeton, NJ: Princeton University Press.

27. Fiorina, Morris, Samuel Abrams, and Jeremy Pope. 2003. "The 2000 US Presidential Election: Can Retrospective Voting Be Saved?" *British Journal of Political Science* 48: 723–741.
28. McClurg, Scott, and Thomas Holbrook. 2009. "Living in a Battleground: Presidential Campaigns and Fundamental Predictors of Vote Choice." *Political Research Quarterly* 62: 495–506.
29. Stimson, James. 2004. *Tides of Consent: How Public Opinion Shapes American Politics*. Cambridge, UK: Cambridge University Press.
30. Hillygus, D. Sunshine, and Simon Jackman. 2003. "Voter Decision Making in Election 2000: Campaign Effects, Partisan Activation, and the Clinton Legacy." *American Journal of Political Science* 47: 583–596.
31. http://www.acgov.org/rov/rcv/faq.htm.
32. http://www.acgov.org/rov/rcv/faq.htm.

10

CONCLUSION

We hope the preceding chapters have provided readers with a solid understanding of how campaigns and elections work. Although we tried to cover a wide range of topics, we recognize that this book is certainly not all inclusive. The study of elections is a rich and diverse area in political science, and it is not possible to cover every topic within the confines of one brief volume. Ultimately, we hope that this book stimulates readers to learn even more about electoral politics. Our aim has been to provide a solid foundation for further inquiry.

In the introductory chapter, we pointed out that ordinary Americans seem to be quite displeased with the way that electoral politics work. Levels of political engagement as well as trust in elected officials and political institutions are remarkably low. Concerns about U.S. elections and campaigns abound. These observations have led many commentators to point out that our system of government is broken. Although we agree that there are many challenges in our current system, we believe Americans can fix much of what's wrong with electoral politics *by working within the current system of institutions*. Our system of government empowers ordinary citizens with a plethora of tools that can be leveraged to improve the electoral process. A centerpiece of the existing political system is that it enables reform of institutions, processes, or behaviors—or all of the above if necessary.

Unfortunately, many people do not engage regularly in political life. Some may withdraw because they perceive the system to be flawed, but it is more likely that the system is flawed *because* too many citizens have withdrawn. It's a vicious cycle. It is difficult to imagine problems being solved without clear cues (intense participation, strong public opinion, etc.) from the public about what they desire. In order to get what they want out of elected officials and government, Americans are going to have to take action to address the concerns they have. In short, there must be consistent and meaningful participation in elections and in the political process once elections are over. There are plenty of tools available within our system that could lead to improvements in the ways elections and campaigns unfold. Most of what people perceive as "broken" within our electoral system can be fixed *if people stop throwing up their arms and start rolling up their sleeves to start the hard work of renewing our democracy.*

On this score, there are reasons for optimism. We find it an encouraging sign, for instance, that growing proportions of Americans report interest in elections overall, with more and more Americans caring who wins presidential contests. Figure 10.1 illustrates these patterns using data from the American National Elections Studies conducted between 1952 and 2012. Surveys conducted in the two or three most recent presidential election cycles register the highest such levels ever observed in these studies. During the most recent election, for example, more than 80% of Americans reported being at least somewhat interested in elections and caring a great deal about the presidential election outcome. It is conceivable that growing partisan polarization explains at least part of these patterns, but taken together with other evidence about rising participation rates in recent cycles (discussed in Chapter 2 above), a portrait of an increasingly engaged electorate clearly emerges. In an era in which election outcomes provide starkly different policy outcomes, the rising mobilization and engagement of citizens is both critical and encouraging. We are hopeful such interest will be sustained, will grow further, and will translate into other realms, including state and local affairs and other aspects of national politics beyond elections. Overall, we interpret these developments to be good news for democracy in America.

A key aim of this volume—in addition to providing a general sense of how elections work—has been to show readers they have tools at their disposal to fix things they dislike about electoral politics. In addition, we hope we have clarified some of the misperceptions about American elections. While aspects of our democracy can be frustrating, it may not be as bad as it seems at first glance. Of course, the fact that our system provides tools to solve the things the public dislikes doesn't mean that those problems can be solved overnight. It could take months, years, or even decades to change elements of the electoral system that are viewed as problematic. It's unlikely that complex issues like campaign finance can be addressed without a great deal of effort and sustained attention. In a society where people have come to expect instantaneous responses, we sometimes need to be reminded that political change often comes

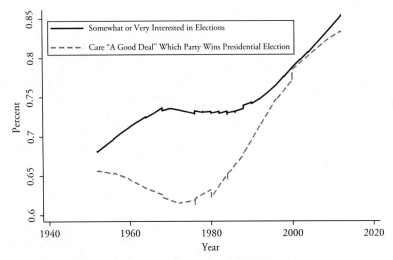

Figure 10.1 Growing Proportions of Americans Report Being at Least "Somewhat Interested" in Elections and Caring "A Good Deal" About Which Party Wins Presidential Elections, 1952–2012. Data from American National Election Studies (http://www.electionstudies.org). Lines are lowess smoothed.

about slowly. If an issue or problem is perceived as important, though, the time investment is likely to be worth it. We recognize that politics is hard work, but we believe sustaining a thriving democracy is worth the cost. We hope that our suggestions at the end of each chapter got readers thinking about the kinds of things that could be changed to create a better system, but these are not necessarily recommendations or prescriptions. They are food for thought, examples of reforms or changes that could be adopted without fundamental or wholesale overhaul of the electoral process.

We also hope that this book has given readers a sense of how the electoral process in the United States provides political representation. Elections are not only critical to establishing representation but also to keeping our leaders' attention focused on citizens' preferences after the election has concluded. In a study of the California state legislature, political scientist James Kuklinksi showed that responsiveness (the degree to which legislators supported issue positions preferred by voters) among state senators serving four-year terms tends to spike as elections approach and then wane following elections, as senators feel insulated until election time rolls around again. By contrast, responsiveness among assembly members in California tends to stay the same over the course of their terms, presumably because they are up for reelection every two years.[1] If the goal of elections is to keep legislators attentive to citizens' wishes, they seem to be doing so, at least to some extent; these findings lend credence to the notion that elections keep elected officials in check, providing powerful incentives for them not to stray too far from what the public truly wants. But whether legislators are adequately attentive and responsive to our preferences as citizens is a question of degree and remains open for debate.

In the end, it is clear that democracy is compromised when the electoral process breaks down. It is our job as citizens to remain vigilant and to take action when necessary to strengthen the democratic process. The good news is that we are empowered to do so, even without fundamental change to the electoral system currently in place. While we acknowledge weaknesses and ample opportunities for improvement, we do not feel it is wise (or necessary) to throw the baby out with the bathwater. Moreover, we must acknowledge that any reforms can have unintended, even harmful, consequences when they are not thoughtfully considered or properly implemented, so change may need to be paced and deliberate. Patience may be as crucial an ingredient as innovation when it comes to sustaining our democracy and the delicate balance that preserves and protects it.

Note

1. Kuklinski, James. 1978. "Relationship between the Temporal Proximity of Elections and Representativeness of California State Legislators." *American Political Science Review* 72: 174.

INDEX